LOUIS PASTEUR

HUNTING KILLER GERMS

IDEAS ON TRIAL

LOUIS PASTEUR
HUNTING KILLER GERMS

E. A. M. Jakab

McGraw-Hill

New York St. Louis San Francisco Auckland Bogotá Caracas
Lisbon London Madrid Mexico City Milan Montreal
New Delhi San Juan Singapore Sydney Tokyo Toronto

A Bank Street Biography

For my parents and for my brother

Ideas on Trial

The *Ideas on Trial* series presents dramatic stories of men and women in science and medicine who waged heroic struggles and risked their comfort, freedom, reputations, and sometimes their lives, for the sake of pursuing their work.

The authors use a docu-drama, "you are there" style to tell these exciting stories. Wherever possible, actual reported scenes and dialog are used, along with quotes from letters, diaries, newspapers, and journals of the time. In a few cases, however, the authors had to invent scenes and dialog for events that did occur, but for which there was no reported scene or dialog.

---

1 2 3 4 5 6 7 8 9 0 DOC/DOC 0 9 8 7 6 5 4 3 2 1 0

ISBN 0-07-134334-2

The Bank Street Series Project Editor was Elisabeth Jakab. The Developmental Editor was Mary Loebig Giles.

The sponsoring editor for this book was Griffin Hansbury, the editing supervisor was Maureen B. Walker, and the production supervisor was Charles H. Annis. The cover and text were designed and set in New Century Schoolbook by Marsha Cohen/ Parallelogram Graphics.

CONTENTS

1

CAN PASTEUR'S RABIES VACCINE FOR DOGS SAVE YOUNG JOSEPH MEISTER?

"Please! I must see Monsieur Pasteur! It is a matter of life and death!"

Outside in the hallway, a woman's voice rang through the hot summer air. Pasteur could even hear footsteps clattering along the corridor of the large, remodeled old building on the outskirts of Paris that served as his laboratory. It was July 6, 1885.

"You cannot disturb Monsieur Pasteur!" cried another voice.

The elderly scientist hurriedly left his microscope and stepped into the hall. He saw several of his assistants trying to get three people to leave.

Joseph Meister in 1885. (The Burndy Library, Dibner Institute for the History of Science and Technology.)

One of the intruders was a nine-year-old boy named Joseph Meister. His eyes were glassy with fear, and he was grimacing in pain and limping badly. Beside him was his mother, her eyes red from weeping, and a neighbor, Monsieur Vone.

"Please! We have travelled on the train for two days from our village to see Monsieur Pasteur!" shouted Monsieur Vone.

Then Madame Meister saw that Pasteur was in the hall.

"Monsieur Pasteur, I ask your help for my son, most urgently, desperately," she pleaded, as an assistant took her arm.

Pasteur waved the assistants away. "I will see them," he said, ushering the three people into his laboratory.

"Now, my child, what is the matter?" Pasteur gently asked the boy. But the child was too frightened to speak.

"A rabid dog attacked and bit him on his way to school," explained Monsieur Vone. "It was my own dog. I had to shoot him."

Pasteur quickly examined Joseph and saw with horror that his hands, arms, and legs were covered with deep, gaping bites—fourteen in all.

Madame Meister began to sob again as she explained how the village doctor had burned Joseph's wounds with carbolic acid.

Pasteur winced at the thought of this small boy undergoing this painful treatment. But he knew that if such a cauterization was done right away, it sometimes prevented a bitten person from getting rabies.

"But it was 12 hours before we could get him to the doctor," Madame Meister went on. "He said that so late after the attack, the acid probably wouldn't help, but that he

Cauterization

Cauterization is burning a wound to prevent infection. In Pasteur's day, a doctor did this with carbolic acid, which was produced by distilling (a method of boiling something down) substances such as wood or coal tar. The acid ate away at the torn flesh, or "burned" it. The village blacksmith also cauterized wounds, but with a hot iron from the fire. In both cases the screaming victim usually had to be held down. Neither treatment was very successful.

heard you developed a vaccine to save dogs from rabies. He thought maybe you could save Joseph too."

"But I've never used my vaccine on a human being!" protested Pasteur. Then he looked again at the sad and desperate faces before him. He knew he had to help.

Pasteur quickly sent some assistants to find two of his colleagues, Monsieur Vulpian, a scientist, and Dr. Grancher, a physician. Both were familiar with his work and came immediately to examine Joseph.

"The boy will surely die if nothing is done," said Dr. Grancher in private afterwards. "The bites are very deep and the skin is broken."

"The carbolic acid was applied too late to do any good. His only hope is your series of rabies inoculations," added Monsieur Vulpian.

"But it could also kill him!" exclaimed Pasteur. "I have no evidence yet that it will work on humans. My staff and I have spent five long years developing this vaccine. And I

The Nightmare of a Death by Rabies

Since ancient times, rabies had been a threat to both humans and animals. Caused by a virus, it was almost always fatal. Mostly wolves, foxes, dogs, and other small mammals caught it. People were infected when a sick animal attacked and bit them. The virus in the animal's saliva quickly entered the person's bloodstream. Once the virus spread from there to the brain, a slow, painful, and horrible death was certain.

Rabies used to be known as Hydrophobia (Latin for "fear of water": hydro = water, phobia = fear) because the victim dreaded the sight of water. It made him want to swallow. But trying to swallow caused unstoppable, painful throat spasms. As a result, the person began to "froth at the mouth"—churning up tiny bubbles of saliva produced by the throat spasms. The victim usually suffocated from all the saliva. The dying patient also suffered from agonizing convulsions, muscle spasms, and periodically flew into uncontrollable fits of mindless rage — that is, he became "rabid."

have lost count of how many poor dogs died from our experiments before we succeeded."

The three men fell silent. Pasteur was right.

If Joseph was given the vaccine and died, Pasteur could be charged with murder.

It didn't matter that without the vaccine, Joseph would die anyway. Pasteur's reputation and career would be

How Pasteur's 1885 Dog Rabies Vaccine Worked

Fourteen injections were given over a ten-day period. The first injection was the weakest: serum made from the spinal cord of a rabid rabbit that died 14 days before. The second dose was made from a 13-day-old spinal cord. And so on down to the last dose, which was made from a one-day-old cord.

The theory behind the treatment was to slowly strengthen the body's immune system until it could totally resist the rabies virus. By overcoming the first and weakest dose, Joseph's body should gain the strength to fight off the second, slightly stronger dose. Then the third, fourth, and rest of the increasingly stronger doses. Finally he would get the last, strongest, and most dangerous dose — one that could kill him.

ruined. His many scientific triumphs would count for nothing. And his enemies would attack him like the mad dogs whose lives he saved with his vaccine.

"My friends," said Pasteur, breaking the silence, "as you know, I intended to begin work on a vaccine for humans. But today, Fate has intervened. A child's life is at stake. And his only hope is *this* vaccine."

He started Joseph on the ten-day series of inoculations at once.

The boy burst into howls of terror as he saw Dr. Grancher prepare a hypodermic needle.

Pasteur tried to comfort him. "There, there, it is nothing, really."

And it was.

"Is that all?" asked Joseph, wiping away his tears. "Why I only felt a pinprick."

Pasteur arranged for Joseph and his mother to stay in a nearby building, and sent Monsieur Vone back home. In ten days, he assured them, Joseph would be out of danger.

But Pasteur was not as sure of that as he seemed. He couldn't sleep all night because he worried so much. Had he done the right thing? What if he was only pounding the last nail into the poor child's coffin?

Each day Pasteur put on a confident face as he supervised Dr. Grancher in giving Joseph the next inoculation. But each night, he spent sleepless hours tossing in bed, alternating between despair and hope. Sometimes he got dressed in the middle of the night and went to see the sleeping child. Joseph would wake up in the morning to see

"Dear Monsieur Pasteur," as he called him, sitting by his bed, anxiously staring at him.

Madame Pasteur wrote their two grown-up children, "Your father has had another bad night; yet there can be no turning back now!"

But while Pasteur worried, Joseph was enjoying himself. His bite wounds were healing, and the injections were nothing to be afraid of. One of Pasteur's assistants took him on outings to a nearby park. He enjoyed playing with the rabbits and guinea pigs in the laboratory; Pasteur even gave him a few of them as pets. He chattered happily about home with Pasteur, who also spent his childhood in a small village.

When Pasteur left to go home, he couldn't help wondering yet again if the boy would live to enjoy a happy childhood in his home village, as Pasteur had in his.

But rabies had been a terrifying deadly threat in Pasteur's home town, too, as he had discovered when he was only eight years old — younger than Joseph.

2

THE RABID WOLF OF ARBOIS

It was a brisk sunny October afternoon in 1831 in the tiny village of Arbois. Eight-year-old Louis Pasteur and his best friend Jules Vercel were playing as they made their way home from school. They chased each other into the woods, over rough farm fences, then back onto the road. As they neared their houses, they suddenly heard screaming and shouting.

"Did someone die?" cried Jules.

"Over there!" exclaimed Louis, pointing toward the blacksmith's shop. A crowd had already gathered.

The boys ran over. Everyone was talking about nine farmers who had been bitten by a rabid wolf.

"Terrible! They'll die for sure!" said one man.

"Maybe not if the blacksmith can help!" said another.

Jules looked at Louis in horror. "We could have been bitten too! We were playing in the woods!" he whispered.

Louis' eyes widened. "Look!" he said.

"Oh no!" said Jules.

Two burly townsmen held the arms of a farmer named Nicole. The blacksmith pulled a red hot iron from the fire and thrust it onto a bloody gash on Nicole's bare shoulder. Nicole screamed. Louis could hear the iron sizzle on his flesh. The farmer twisted and writhed in agony as his two friends struggled to hold him.

"It is over, Nicole," said one of the men holding him. They led him away. "We'll bandage that up right away," said the other.

Another farmer came forward. He had bite wounds on both arms.

The house in Arbois where Pasteur grew up. (© Institut Pasteur, Paris.)

"Louis, you cannot stay here," said a familiar voice. Louis looked up. It was his mother. And there was Jules' mother too. As the women led the boys away, there was a scream. Then a second.

Louis heard a villager say: "This treatment doesn't always work."

"For these poor farmers' sakes, let us hope it does," said another. "Rabies is such a horrible death — fits and screams, terrible pain and madness."

"Say, this is no place for children," a man said as he noticed the boys.

"That is why we are taking them home," replied Madame Pasteur.

Several months later, the boys heard that all the farmers except Nicole died an agonizing death.

"That wolf came right out of the woods to bite them," said a frightened Jules. "We have to be on guard wherever we go!"

He was right, thought Louis. Many wolves roamed all around this countryside. Almost anywhere you went, a wolf could be lurking.

Louis was scared, but he was also curious. At dinner, his three sisters stared in surprise as he asked his parents why the bite of a mad wolf could make someone die. "And why does burning the wound save some people and not others?" he went on.

No one had any answers, his father told him. "The mad wolf gives the madness to anyone he bites. That is all we know."

His mother added that rabies had been feared since ancient times. "No one knows what causes it," she said. "Perhaps no one ever will."

Louis shivered. It was as if rabies were some kind of deadly curse.

The danger of rabid wolves aside, Louis' life in Arbois was a safe and happy one. His family was warm and loving. As a teenager, he liked to draw and made some very good portraits of his parents and friends. And, although he was small for his age and not very strong, Louis also liked to help his father. Jean Joseph Pasteur was a tanner, a person who took animal skins and turned them into leather. Louis was fascinated by how this happened.

"First, we leave the cattle hides soaking in the lime for a while," instructed his father. Made from limestone or shells, the smelly lime ate away at the hides, making them softer and loosening the hair.

Afterwards, Louis and his father rinsed the lime off the hides and scraped off any hair that was left. Then they spread even smellier chicken manure on the hides.

"It stinks!" exclaimed Louis.

"It does the job," said his father.

Once the manure was finally removed, Louis helped his father put the hides into a pit and cover them with dried, shredded oak bark. That was pretty smelly too, he thought.

After being covered with the oak bark for a time, the rough animal hide turned into a smooth piece of leather. *How did this happen?* wondered Louis. His father couldn't tell him. He only knew the process worked, and that tan-

How the Manure and the Oak Bark Worked

The manure contained microbes, tiny living organisms, that ate up the stiff material between the hide's inner fibers. At that time, almost no one thought that such things as microbes existed. The oak bark contained tannin (a chemical that also occurs in tea bushes and other plants). The tannin seeped out of the oak bark and into the empty spaces between the fibers in the hide, making it both soft and strong.

ners had always done it this way. *How I would like to know!* thought Louis. *Maybe some day I will find out.*

Although Louis was always ready to help in the tannery, Jean Joseph knew how much more his son enjoyed his schoolwork. He urged Louis not to become a tanner, but to think of becoming a teacher.

Louis was uncertain. "Some of my teachers say I am slow," he said.

"That is only because you are so thorough," said his father.

One day, when he was fifteen, Louis rushed home from school.

"The headmaster says I should go to a higher school for two or three more years to prepare for the entrance exams

The History of the Pasteur Family

Although generations of Pasteurs had been tanners, in his youth Jean Joseph rose to become a sergeant in Napoleon's army. Napoleon personally awarded him the Legion of Honor for bravery.

The Pasteurs had come a long way. Jean Joseph's great-grandfather, Claude Pasteur, was a serf. Serfdom was a kind of slavery that was widespread in Europe and Russia. At the age of 30, in 1763, Claude bought his freedom — and the freedom of his descendants — for four pieces of gold. Serfdom finally was abolished in 1789 in France.

for the Ecole Normale Supérieure in Paris!" he exclaimed to his parents. The Ecole was the best university in all of France.

His parents were thrilled the headmaster thought so highly of Louis. Then his father's face fell. There were no higher schools in Arbois. Louis would have to move away from home; he would need money not only for tuition but for room and board.

"Almost all of our income goes to support the six of us," Louis' father said. And one of Louis' sisters was mentally retarded because of an illness she had at the age of three. She would always have to be taken care of.

"Don't worry, we will find a way to afford this," said Madame Pasteur.

It was a struggle, but they did. Louis was able to pay for part of his tuition (and later on, all of it) by teaching classes of younger students. His father paid for the rest.

In the fall of 1843, the authorities at the Ecole were startled by a young man who arrived several days before the term began.

"I am Louis Pasteur," he told them. "I came in fourth in the national exams." He wanted permission to take up residence in the empty dormitory.

"What an eager student," they said, and let him stay.

He spent the time reading books on chemistry. He had never been so happy. At last he was on the way to finding out how the chemical processes that fascinated him as a child worked. Perhaps some day he would also find out why the rabid wolf of Arbois was able to kill so many farmers.

3

SOLVING THE MYSTERY OF THE CRYSTALS

In May 1848, less than a year after he graduated from the Ecole Normale with his doctorate, the 25-year-old Pasteur solved an important scientific mystery while working as a laboratory assistant to Antoine Balard, a famous professor at the Ecole. He was so excited that he rushed out of the laboratory and grabbed the first person he saw, another lab assistant.

"I have just made a great discovery!" he told the startled youth. "I must tell you all about it!" He did so in a nearby park, the Luxembourg Gardens.

Here is what happened: A famous German chemist had discovered that two types of living (organic) crystal acids were identical chemically. But they acted differently when he studied them in a liquid (in solution) under the microscope. One of them, tartrate crystals, rotated light to the

Pasteur as a student at L'Ecole Normale Supérieure in Paris.
(© Institut Pasteur, Paris.)

right. The other, paratartrate crystals, had no effect on light at all. Pasteur couldn't get this odd chemical mystery out of his mind. What a coup if he, a young chemist barely out of school, could solve it!

First, he examined tartrate crystals under his microscope. The crystals were an uneven shape (asymmetrical). Pasteur had an idea: *what if the crystals of the paratartrate were even* (symmetrical)? That might explain why they had no effect on light! Eagerly, he got to work. But when he examined the paratartrate crystals, he found they were asymmetrical, too, just like the tartrate crystals. What a disappointment! After all his work!

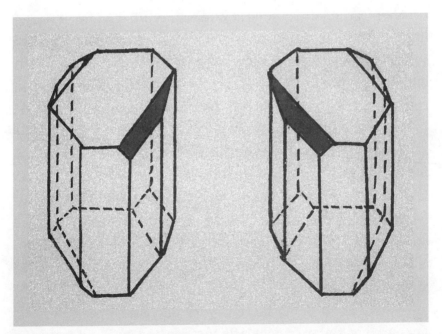

Drawings of the right-handed and left-handed acid crystals that Pasteur published in 1850. (© Institut Pasteur, Paris.)

But Pasteur did not give up. There had to be an answer to the mystery, even if it wasn't *his* answer. He kept examining the tiny crystals, each the size of a grain of beach sand. At last, his eyes aching, his body stiff, he noticed that the crystals were not all alike. Some were "right handed," others "left handed." The "handedness" of crystals was a relatively recent discovery in chemistry. Those rotating light to the right were considered "right handed." "Left-handed" crystals rotated light to the left.

Greatly excited, Pasteur sorted the miniscule crystals one by one with tweezers into two piles, one all right handed, the other all left handed. It took hours. Both piles were about the same size. Then he did three experiments.

He put the left-handed crystals in solution. They rotated light to the left. Then he put the right-handed crystals in solution. They rotated light to the right. Finally, he put both batches together. They had no effect on light. The left- and right-handed crystals canceled each other out!

He had solved the mystery!

Professor Balard was thrilled when he learned Pasteur had made such a fundamental discovery. At this time, no one knew that a substance could have both left- and right-handed crystals. Nor that the two types would cancel each other out optically. "You must write a report on this for the Academy of Sciences," Professor Balard told Louis. "This feat will make your name!"

But a week or so later a very sad and upset Pasteur appeared at Balard's door. His mother had suffered a stroke, the sudden breaking or blockage of a blood vessel in the brain.

"She died before I could get home." Tears welled up in his eyes. "I cannot even think about work right now," he said. He had to go home to be with his father and sisters in Arbois for a while.

When Pasteur returned to Paris several weeks later, he discovered Balard had spread the news about his discovery. The grand old man of science, the famous Jean-Baptiste Biot, was skeptical. "I should like to examine closely that young man's results," he said. It was Biot who had discovered that it was the particular kind of asymmetry (unevenness) of crystals that made them left or right handed.

A somewhat nervous Pasteur performed the same experiment under Biot's stern supervision. When the results turned out to be exactly the same, the astounded Biot took him by the arms and said, "My dear boy, I have loved science so much all my life that this stirs my very heart." From that day on he treated Pasteur like a son. He and Balard helped

A Fundamental Scientific Discovery

Pasteur's research on the paratartrate crystals helped lead to the development of the modern science of stereochemistry, which deals with the spacial relationships of molecules.

Pasteur get a job as an Assistant Professor of Chemistry at the University of Strasbourg.

In Strasbourg, the 26-year-old Pasteur, the careful student who took his time about everything, fell in love at first sight. He paid a courtesy call on the rector of the University, Monsieur Laurent, and met his 22-year-old daughter, Marie. The couple were married five months later. Marie was fascinated by Louis' work. "You must teach me about everything, so I can help you," she said. In the years to come, she would be his closest friend, a laboratory assistant, sounding board, editor, and secretary. As Pasteur's assistant, Emile Roux, was to write many years later, "Madame Pasteur was more than an incomparable companion for her husband, she was his best collaborator."

During the four years the Pasteurs remained in Strasbourg, their happiness was increased by the birth of three children: Jeanne in 1850; Jean-Baptiste in 1851; and Cécile in 1853. Pasteur was a devoted father.

Pasteur continued his research on crystals but in a different direction. He realized that the asymmetry (unevenness) and "handedness" of crystals in solution was only found in living (organic) matter. He tried feverishly to create life itself by doing experiments to transform the symmetric (even) molecules of a non-living substance into asymmetric living ones. He failed, again and again. He even wrote his father, "someone would have to be a little crazy to keep trying to do what I am doing!" Pasteur finally gave up. (Even today, scientists have come nowhere near to accomplishing this!) By now, 1853, Pasteur was more and more interested in the teeming invisible world he saw under his microscope. What effect did these tiny living things have on the visible world he lived in? Could some of them cause disease?

Pasteur's Scientific Method

In the fall of 1854, Pasteur became Professor of Chemistry and Dean at the new School of Sciences at Lille. At the opening ceremonies he spoke about how important hard work and study were to a scientist in making discoveries.

"Chance favors only the mind that is prepared," he said. He meant that while there were plenty of "accidents" in science, there were no "accidental" discoveries. It was only as a result of years of study and experimentation that the "prepared mind" was able to figure out what the "accident" meant.

Pasteur was not only describing the nature of scientific method, he was describing himself.

4

THE PUZZLE OF THE SPOILING BEET JUICE

"Here is that Pasteur again, he'll be asking us lots more questions, I bet," grumbled one of the workers in the beet juice factory in Lille.

"I hear he takes his students on trips to all kinds of factories, to steel mills and metal works," said another. "Who ever heard of such a thing!"

"Let's hope he doesn't bring them here!"

As usual, the young chemistry professor walked around eagerly inspecting everything and asking questions. He didn't seem to care if he got his fine clothes dirty. He stepped right up to a big vat of fresh beet juice and watched the workers add a small blob of yellowish yeast to it. The yeast immediately began to dissolve. The yeast would slowly form a thin mold over the top of the liquid. Then little bubbles would start popping up. This was fermentation, the process which gradually transformed the beet juice into alcohol.

But the reason Pasteur was here was that lately the beet juice was spoiling instead of turning into alcohol. And not only at this factory but many others in Lille as well. Monsieur Bigo, the owner of the factory and the father of one of Pasteur's students, had asked for his help.

Day after day Pasteur returned to the factory. He took samples of the juice, filtered and unfiltered, spoiled and unspoiled. He also took samples of the thicker sludge in the vats. He carefully studied everything under the microscope in his laboratory.

Finally, one day weeks later, after he had analyzed dozens of samples, he discovered small round particles in the unspoiled juice. In the spoiled juice, he found much smaller rod-shaped particles. These particles must be living things that somehow made the beet juice turn bad, he thought.

Pasteur didn't know why or how these particles occurred—yet. But he did know he had a quick and practical remedy for Monsieur Bigo and the other factory owners.

"You must regularly look at samples from each vat under a microscope," he told Monsieur Bigo. "If you see round particles in the liquid, the beet juice will ferment properly. But if you see rod-shaped particles, the juice will spoil and you must throw it out."

Fascinated by what he had discovered in the beet vats, Pasteur began to study fermentation. Most scientists believed it was purely a chemical process, that is, nonorganic chemicals reacting to each other. Pasteur was not so sure. A few years later, in the summer of 1857, he made a strange discovery. During the warm weather, one of his lab-

The Ferment over Fermentation

Fermenting agents bring about biological change. For instance, decay is a type of fermentation too.

Although people had used fermentation since ancient times to make bread, cheese, vinegar, alcohol and alcoholic drinks, in Pasteur's time no one understood much about it.

Germany's leading chemist, Justus von Liebig, declared fermentation was only a chemical reaction, the generally accepted view. A few scientists believed fermenting agents contained living particles that made fermentation happen. Pasteur was one of them. Besides studying alcoholic fermentation, Pasteur began to study lactic acid fermentation, used to make butter and cheese. (The rod-shaped particles that spoiled the beet juice turned out to be lactic acid — the wrong ferment for turning beet juice into alcohol.)

If Pasteur could isolate a type of living organism (a microbe) and prove that it caused only one type of fermentation, he would be on his way to proving that other types of microbes caused other kinds of fermentation.

Pasteur in 1857, while Dean of the Faculté des sciences at Lille. (© Institut Pasteur, Paris.)

oratory solutions got a mold on it. A mold was the first stage in the fermentation process. Pasteur decided to find out how a mold would act on the organic crystals in paratartrate acid (the same acid in which he had discovered both right- and left-handed crystals). To his amazement, the mold destroyed—or "fed upon"—the right-handed crystals, but ignored the left-handed ones. As a result of this, he decided that fermenting agents were definitely living organisms, not chemical reactions.

In October, the Pasteurs returned to Paris. Louis was now Director of Scientific Studies and Administrator at the Ecole Normale Supérieure. It was a big honor for such a young man. Louis was not yet 35 years old. He was happy about his new job, but what he was most interested in now was fermentation. He was sure that solving its mysteries would lead to other discoveries, maybe even to the causes of animal and human diseases.

5

THE GREAT DEBATE: CAN LIFE ARISE FROM NOTHING?

"Hmmph!" snorted Pasteur as he sat at home one night in December 1858. He was reading a report presented to the Academy of Sciences by Felix Pouchet, the Director of the Natural History Museum in Rouen.

"What is it, Louis?" asked Marie, looking up from her book.

"Monsieur Pouchet claims he has proved the doctrine of Spontaneous Generation," Pasteur replied as he underlined parts of the report.

"And you don't think he has."

"I don't believe in his test results. I am going to check his statements with my own experiments," said Pasteur.

Something from Nothing

The doctrine of Spontaneous Generation, the idea that life could arise from nothing, without any "parents" or cause, had been around for thousands of years. It was a handy way to explain the sudden appearance of living things that seemed to pop up from nowhere. People thought eels were generated spontaneously out of mud; maggots from rotting meat; and frogs, snails, and leeches from swampy mists. To generate mice, they said, all you had to do was put down old rags with some corn, and in 21 days the corn would turn into mice. By the 19th century, many scientists had abandoned this doctrine, but many others still supported it.

Marie grinned. "Well, in that case, I think it is very fortunate that you finally managed to get your own laboratory."

Pasteur laughed.

The authorities at the Ecole Normale had refused to give him a laboratory. They wanted him to concentrate on being an administrator, not a scientist. But Pasteur found two tiny empty rooms five flights up in the Ecole Normale attic. The ceiling was so low he had to bend over a little, but the place would do. After he swept out the dust and cobwebs, Marie helped him furnish it.

A few weeks after he read Pouchet's report, Pasteur received a letter from Pouchet, who knew that Pasteur's work on fermentation might contradict Pouchet's findings. Pouchet challenged Pasteur to accept his experimental results. He claimed Pasteur should do this because he had proved once and for all that Spontaneous Generation was real. Pasteur wrote back that he believed Pouchet was wrong and that he would prove it.

What Pasteur had to do was to prove that fermentation was caused by a living organism—that is, he had to discover a cause for what Pouchet was insisting had no cause.

In August, Pasteur put his research on hold to take care of 8-year-old Jean-Baptise and 6-year-old Cecile. Madame Pasteur, taking their one-year-old baby Marie Louise with her, rushed to Arbois to nurse 9-year-old Jeanne. She had caught typhoid fever while visiting her grandfather.

Back in Paris, Pasteur waited anxiously for news. He was relieved when Marie wrote that Jeanne was improving. But then Jeanne took a sudden turn for the worse and died early in September before her father could reach Arbois. Her parents were crushed and full of grief. Later that year Pasteur wrote his father, "I cannot keep my thoughts from my poor little girl, so good, so happy in her little life, whom this fatal year has taken away from us." *Why couldn't the doctors save her?* he wondered bitterly.

The grieving father turned back to his work. One day he had an inspired idea. What if the air itself was full of microbes, tiny living organisms that were invisible to people? What if they floated down along with the endless stream of tiny dust specks a person can see floating through a sunbeam? The microbes would land on everything, organ-

Death and Disease in the 19th Century

Death from disease in childhood was common in Europe. Statistics show that one out of four children died before the age of two. Medicine was primitive compared to today. A standard treatment was using blood-sucking worms called leeches to bleed patients — which usually did no good and only made them weaker from loss of blood. Doctors often could not help and sometimes were not even sure what illness a patient had. People could get sick and die in a day or two without anyone knowing why.

Hygiene didn't exist; open sewers and contaminated water were common. Doctors never washed their hands before treating a patient, no matter how bloody they were from the previous patient. They merely wiped their hands on their white coats.

In Pasteur's family, an older brother died shortly after birth, and a sister was retarded as a result of a disease she caught at age three.

Adults were hardly immune from disease either. Pasteur's middle sister died suddenly the year after he was married. His third sister got sick and died within 48 hours when Pasteur was 58.

ic and inorganic alike. But if they landed on organic substances, the microbes would feed on them and thus be able to grow and multiply. They might even cause changes such as fermentation. Even decay. Perhaps even disease.

Therefore, there could be no such thing as Spontaneous Generation, he decided. Life could only arise from life. Every living thing had a living cause or "parent." All he had to do was prove it.

One day Pasteur's old boss, Professor Balard, visited to see how Pasteur was coming with proving Spontaneous Generation did not exist.

"I have done it," said Pasteur. First, he had sterilized sugared yeast water by boiling it to kill any microbes or other living matter in it. Then he poured it into flasks, heating the air in the flasks to make the air sterile too. Then he sealed the flasks and waited for Spontaneous Generation to happen.

Nothing happened, not even when the flasks were left for weeks.

Finally one day he unsealed a flask and let in ordinary air. In two days, the water became cloudy, with thin little threads. When he put a few drops under the microscope, he saw bacteria, molds, and other sorts of microbes.

"You have done it indeed!" exclaimed Balard proudly.

"One problem remains," said Pasteur unhappily.

He explained that believers in Spontaneous Generation also believed the air contained a "life force" which helped cause Spontaneous Generation. They would say that when Pasteur sterilized the air, he killed the "life force."

"I have to prove my theory with ordinary air," said Pasteur.

"What if you use a swan neck flask? " asked Balard with a smile.

"That is it! Thank you!" exclaimed Pasteur. He began work at once.

After he put some yeast water in a flask, he heated the neck of the flask until the glass began to melt. Using a pair of tongs, he pulled out the neck to form a long thin tube that he first curved downward, then gently upward. Then he boiled the flask to kill microbes in the water as well as in the air. But since the flask was left unsealed, ordinary air rushed into it as it cooled. But because of the dip in the swan neck, the invisible microbes in this ordinary air got stuck. They could not rise up along the upward curve of the swan neck.

Pasteur made several such flasks, and waited for the "life force" to produce Spontaneous Generation. Weeks passed, and nothing happened. One day he tilted one of the flasks for a second, so some of the trapped microbes in the dip of the swan neck could fall into the liquid. In a day or two, the water became cloudy and little threads appeared.

Both Marie and Balard felt Pasteur had nothing left to prove, but he insisted on doing one more experiment. If the doctrine of Spontaneous Generation *were* true, then microbes would grow anywhere.

"But if they exist in the dust in the air, as I believe they do, there will be more of them in some places than in others," Pasteur told them.

And so, during most of 1860, Pasteur went from place to place in Paris carrying small sealed flasks of sterile yeast water and no air. (He boiled the flask long enough to steam all the air out, creating a vacuum.) To do a test, he broke open the neck of a flask, let the air rush into the vacuum, then sealed it shut again with a portable lamp flame. He took the flasks back to his laboratory and waited. All the air samples from crowded places quickly produced microbes.

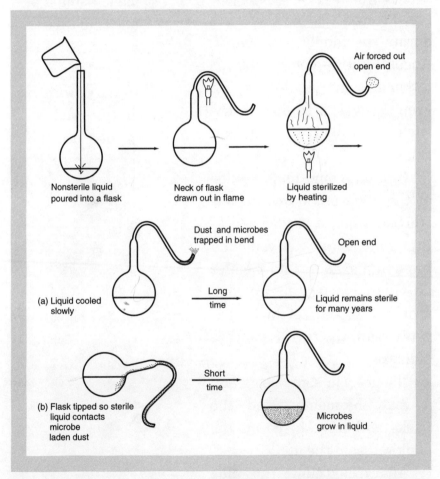

How Pasteur's swan-necked flasks worked. (Redrawn after Dubos, René, "Pasteur and Modern Science," © 1998 American Society for Microbiology.)

Only one of ten flasks opened in the dank, dark cellar of the Paris Observatory, where almost no one ever went, produced microbes.

Being a very thorough person, Pasteur also took samples during the family vacation, in August and September, at his father's home in Arbois. He even decided to go up into the Alps, the nearby mountain range.

One sunny morning, a guide at the town of Chamonix was startled when a studious-looking gentleman arrived and hired him to go up into the Mer de Glace glacier, an ice field that was 6,600 feet high. The gentleman was carrying a case of flasks.

"I'll get you some boots and a coat, Monsieur. And the flasks will have to go on the donkey," said the guide.

After a long climb, the guide watched in amazement as Pasteur broke open flask after

A nineteenth-century artist's depiction of Pasteur on the Mer de Glace glacier. (© Institut Pasteur, Paris.)

flask in the cold fresh air, and then sealed each one with his portable lamp flame.

Pasteur explained he was doing an experiment, but the guide only shook his head.

Only one of the 20 flasks Pasteur opened on the glacier produced microbes. His theory was proving to be correct. There was no such thing as Spontaneous Generation.

When Pouchet heard about Pasteur's activities, he called on two of his colleagues to help him prove Pasteur wrong.

"We will beat that Pasteur at his own game," he said.

The three men used the same kind of flasks as Pasteur, but with hay in water as the flask liquid. They rushed from place to place, taking their own samples. They even went up La Maladetta, a glacier in the Pyrenees mountain range. At 10,580 feet, it was some 4,000 feet higher than Pasteur's glacier.

"I will prove, again, that Spontaneous Generation exists," said Pouchet.

Suddenly, one of his friends slipped and began tumbling down toward an icy cliff.

"Help!" he cried, flailing his arms helplessly. A guide grabbed him before he could slip over the edge.

Once they were safely back down the mountain, Pouchet and his friends felt triumphant. Everywhere they had gone, microbes grew in their flasks. Therefore, Pasteur was mistaken. They spread the word that they had proved the doctrine of Spontaneous Generation.

When Pasteur heard of this claim, he said that microbes

Pouchet's Mistake

Pasteur was right. Pouchet and his friends had not done their experiments properly. But it was an honest mistake. Pouchet's hay in water was boiled to get rid of all organisms. But what was not known during Pasteur's time was that a certain kind of microbe in hay survives boiling. As a result, Pouchet's "sterile" flasks contained living microbes in a vacuum. These microbes began to grow as soon as fresh air was let in, whether or not that air contained any microbes of its own.

were growing in their flasks only because they had not done their experiments correctly.

Pouchet said Pasteur was wrong. Pasteur said Pouchet was wrong. The debate continued.

On April 7, 1864, Pasteur gave a lecture at the Sorbonne debunking Spontaneous Generation. It was a crowded event. The debate had aroused a great deal of public as well as scientific interest. Besides students and professors, the audience included many celebrities and ordinary people.

Pasteur displayed one of his swan-neck flasks from 1859. Five years later, it was still free of microbes even though ordinary air could get in.

There was no activity in the flask announced Pasteur, "because I have kept it from the only thing man does not know how to produce: from the germs which float in the air, from Life, for *Life is a germ and a germ is Life.*"

Finally, the Academy of Sciences decided to settle the debate about Spontaneous Generation once and for all. They asked Pasteur and Pouchet to appear before a special committee on June 22. Each of them would argue his case and repeat some of their experiments. Then the committee would decide.

Pasteur arrived armed with several of his flasks from his 1860 trip into the Alps. The liquid was still clear.

But Pouchet and his colleagues sent word they would not appear.

Pasteur at work in his laboratory. (© Institut Pasteur, Paris.)

Pasteur won the debate by default.

Back in his laboratory, Pasteur began to consider doing even more research on microbes — and on the diseases they might cause. Perhaps he could find a way to fight the microbes that were deadly. Then children like his beloved little daughter Jeanne would not die.

Life without Oxygen

In 1860, Pasteur accidentally discovered that the microbes causing the fermentation of butyric acid (the acid produced when butter spoils) live without air, but die if air reaches them. The idea that life could exist without oxygen was an astounding and revolutionary discovery, but one that many people refused to believe for a long time.

After consulting the Ecole's Greek professor, Pasteur coined the term *anaerobic* (an = not; aero = air; bic, from bios = life) to describe these microbes. He described microbes that needed air to live as *aerobic*.

Pasteur also found that the microbes causing decay were anaerobic. This would help him later on with his research on a vaccine for anthrax.

6

CURING THE "SICK" WINES OF FRANCE

"Hello, Louis, are you there?" It was Jules Vercel, Pasteur's childhood friend. As boys, they had seen the village blacksmith use a red-hot iron to burn the rabid wolf bites of the farmer Nicole.

On this sunny September morning in 1864, Vercel arrived to meet his friend at an old building outside of Arbois which Pasteur and his assistants had set up as a laboratory. The Pasteurs and their four children (including one-year-old baby Camille) were on vacation, staying with Pasteur's father. But for Pasteur, vacation meant a chance to work on another problem. This time it was spoiled wine. The Emperor Napoleon III himself had asked Pasteur to find a cure for the "wine diseases" that were ruining many French wines. Famous all over the world, the wines were one of the country's major exports. It was Pasteur's patriotic duty to find a cure.

Pasteur was delighted to see his old friend. He was also delighted to see what Vercel was carrying.

"I brought you samples of the spoiled wines from my vineyard. The other winemakers will do the same," said Vercel.

Vercel followed Pasteur inside the building, where the laboratory assistants immediately took charge of the spoiled wine.

"Do you really believe you can find out what is wrong with our wines by looking at them under a microscope?" asked Vercel with a smile. *How could Pasteur help?* he wondered. He didn't even know how to make wine.

"I have some ideas already," said Pasteur. He explained that he had studied wines for the past few years as part of his research on fermentation.

"The Emperor's request has made me increase my efforts," he said.

"Well, there is no doubt that we need help," said Vercel.

A week or so later, Vercel and some other winemakers watched as Pasteur put a drop of spoiled wine under the microscope and took one look.

"This wine is bitter," he announced.

The winemakers were amazed. How could he know that without tasting the wine? Perhaps it was just a lucky guess.

"Try this wine," said one, handing him a carafe.

Pasteur put a drop under the microscope. "This one is acidic," he said.

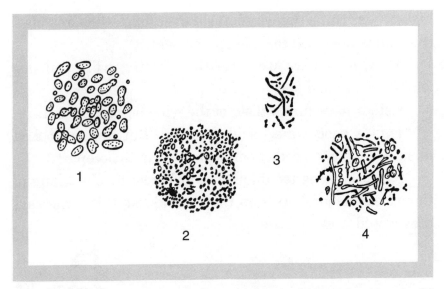

Microbes Pasteur saw with his microscope in (1) healthy wine, in (2) acidic wine, (3) oily wine, and (4) bitter wine. (Redrawn after Burton, Mary June, "Louis Pasteur: Founder of Microbiology.")

Pasteur picked up another carafe and put a drop of that under the microscope. "This one is oily."

He said, "I know what is wrong with the wine without tasting it because I can see the different microbes that make it bitter, acidic, or oily. Now I must find a way to protect your wines from these microbes."

After many weeks of experiments, Pasteur finally was able to tell the winemakers that he had found a way they could "cure" their wines. They must heat the wines at a temperature between 50 and 60 degrees centigrade (122 and 140 degrees Fahrenheit) for a few minutes.

"The heat kills the microbes that spoil your wine. It does not hurt the wine. A lower heat does not kill the microbes. A higher heat ruins the wine's taste by killing other microbes that the wines need to develop," he said.

The winemakers were upset. "Heating will spoil our wines!" exclaimed one.

Pasteur gave him a taste of the wine he had heated.

"This is good wine," said the man. But he still looked unsure. It was too radical an idea for him to accept.

"I will use this technique," said Vercel firmly. Many of the other winemakers said they would too. But some said they would wait and see.

The Triumph of Pasteurization

It took several more demonstrations and trials, but the heating, or "pasteurization," of wine was soon adopted. Pasteur even designed machinery to pasteurize wine. In one of the more dramatic trials of this technique, pasteurized and unpasteurized wine were put aboard a Navy ship going on a ten-month trip. On the ship's return, the pasteurized wine still tasted fine; the unpasteurized wine tasted acidic.

In time, pasteurization was used not only for wines, but also to eliminate spoilage and disease-causing organisms in milk, butter, cheese, cider, vinegar, beer, and other foods.

7

SAVING THE DISEASED SILKWORMS

After curing the "sick" wines of France, Pasteur went back to work on fermentation, eagerly searching for the causes of disease. But once again, the government asked him to help save one of France's major industries.

On a spring day in 1865, a letter arrived from Pasteur's old chemistry professor, the famous Jean-Baptiste Dumas, who was now a Senator. He represented Le Gard, one of France's largest silkgrowing regions.

Pasteur *must* help save the silkworms, wrote Dumas.

The silkworms were dying from an epidemic of pebrine (from the word pebre = pepper), a disease which dotted them with tiny black spots that looked like grains of pepper. The silk industry was nearly in ruins, with losses totaling hundreds of millions of francs. More than 3,600 local officials and silkgrowers signed a petition demanding help from the government. Something had to be done!

Pasteur's drawing of a silk worm. (© Institut Pasteur, Paris.)

When Pasteur replied that he knew nothing about silk-worms and had never even touched one, Dumas wrote back, "So much the better! For ideas, you will have only those which shall come to you as a result of your own observations!"

Pasteur accepted the commission, writing Dumas that "the subject... may even come within the range of my present studies." Pasteur felt that his fermentation research would help him to discover how humans and animals got diseases. But being a chemist, he had little experience with biological problems. Tackling the silkworm disease would give him that experience.

Pasteur's drawing of a silk moth. (© Institut Pasteur, Paris.)

On June 6, 1865, Pasteur departed for Alais, a town in Le Gard near the Mediterranean sea. It was a center of the silk industry. The first thing he discovered was that other scientists who examined the sick silkworms under a microscope sometimes found small, shiny oval cells inside their bodies. They called these tiny cells "corpuscles." Some scientists believed the corpuscles were part of the pebrine disease. Others did not, because sometimes the corpuscles showed up in apparently healthy silkworms.

What confused everyone even more was that some black-spotted silkworms were *not* sick, and some silkworms without any black spots were!

In preparation for his task, Pasteur had learned all he could about silkworms. Their life cycle was about two months, and occured sometime between April and June of every year. After hatching from tiny seedlike eggs, the silkworms lived in groups called broods. The silkworm grew so much — from a tiny seed-sized worm up to as much as 3 inches — that it shed its skin, or molted, four times before it was ready to spin a silk cocoon — a pale-gold, puffy ball — around itself. Inside the cocoon, the silkworm turned into a chrysalis or *pupa,* a kind of hibernating worm, that developed into a moth. The moth broke out of the cocoon and mated. The female then laid between 600 and 800 eggs, and both the male and female moth died.

Every year, the grower let some moths break out of their cocoons so they would produce eggs to hatch the following spring. He harvested the rest of the cocoons by putting them in a steam bath that killed the chrysalis. After the cocoons dried, he unwound the silken thread. The thread could be dyed various colors and then woven into shimmering silk cloth.

But now the diseased silkworms were not spinning good cocoons, or else they died before they finished spinning. Other silkworms died before they even started to spin their cocoons.

By the time Pasteur arrived, the silkworms' life cycle was nearly over. He had to work quickly if he was going to give the growers any help for the next year's cycle.

But most of the growers were skeptical that a "mere chemist" could help them. Why hadn't the government sent someone who really knew something, say a zoologist or a silkworm cultivator, instead?

Pasteur was unfazed by their doubts. "Be patient," he told them. He began interviewing the growers and their workers, and examining silkworms under the microscope.

Then on June 15, he received a telegram that his father had been taken ill. But before he reached Arbois, his father died. The grieving Pasteur wrote to his wife in Paris, "Until the last moment I hoped I should see him again, embrace him for the last time... but when I arrived at the station I saw some of our cousins all in black, coming from Salins; it was only then that I understood that I could but accompany him to the grave."

After the funeral, Pasteur wrote his wife and children, "I long to see you all, but must go back to Alais, for my studies would be retarded by a year if I could not spend a few days there now."

By June 25, Pasteur was able to give the growers some practical advice.

"Isolate each mated pair of moths until the female lays her eggs," he told them. "Then examine both moths under the microscope. If either has corpuscles in its body, the eggs are diseased and must be destroyed. If both moths are free of corpuscles, then the eggs will hatch healthy silkworms."

Many growers took Pasteur's advice. Others grumbled that they didn't like a chemist telling them what to do. "Besides, we won't know if his advice is any good until the silkworm eggs hatch next spring," they said. Dealers in silkworm eggs were particularly angry. If they followed Pasteur's advice, they would have to throw away much of their stock.

When Pasteur finally returned to Paris in early July, he found that two-year-old Camille was seriously ill with a liver disease. Again, the doctors did not seem able to help. The miserable parents took turns sitting by the bedside of their dying child — Marie during the day, Pasteur in the evenings, after his day in the laboratory. Often, he simply held Camille's tiny hand. The little girl died in September. The griefstricken parents buried her in Arbois, beside her grandparents and sister Jeanne.

Pasteur turned back to his work. In February 1866, he and his assistants returned to Alais to continue their silkworm research. They rented a large house at Pont Gisquet, about a mile outside of Alais, and set up a laboratory and silkworm nursery.

In April, Madame Pasteur left Paris with 12-year-old

Cécile and 8-year-old Marie Louise. They were traveling to Alais to spend the Easter holidays with Pasteur. Sixteen-year-old Jean-Baptiste stayed behind because of school.

Along the way, Madame Pasteur and the two girls stopped over in the town of Chambery, where Cécile suddenly fell ill with typhoid fever. Madame Pasteur wrote her husband that they would be delayed a short while. A few days later, she wrote again: Cécile's recovery would take longer than expected. Alarmed, Pasteur hurried to his daughter's bedside. But when he arrived, Cécile seemed to be well on the way to recovery. She was sitting up, smiling and glad to see him. After a few days, the relieved father returned to Alais.

But on May 21, Madame Pasteur sent him a telegram. Cécile had had a sudden relapse. Two days later, before her father could reach Chambery, she died. After the funeral service, Pasteur took her coffin to Arbois, where she was buried next to her grandparents and two sisters.

Pasteur was in despair. He wrote his equally despairing wife, "Our beloved children die one after another!" He felt more helpless than ever against disease. How had he ever thought he could fight it?

Madame Pasteur wrote to Jean-Baptiste that she was not returning to Paris: "I could not leave your poor father to go back to Alais alone after this great sorrow." She and Marie Louise settled in at the Pont Gisquet house.

Pasteur and his assistants continued their research on the silkworms, both in the laboratory and in the silkworm nursery. They produced so many healthy eggs that they were able to give batches of them to the growers. Madame Pasteur and Marie Louise pitched in too. The two of them sorted, counted, and then carefully unravelled the cocoons. Marie Louise even asked to be taught how to examine the silkworms under the microscope. In the evenings, Pasteur dictated his research notes to Madame Pasteur.

One day some growers complained to Pasteur that he could not expect them to learn to use such a complicated instrument as a microscope to look for corpuscles in their silkworms.

Pasteur replied, "There is in my laboratory a little girl eight years of age who has learned to use it without difficulty."

The growers decided they could learn to use the microscope after all.

A few weeks later, Pasteur hurriedly called the growers together.

"You must separate the sick worms from the healthy ones as quickly as possible!" he told them.

As a result of his observations, Pasteur had discovered that pebrine was highly contagious. A healthy worm that came in any kind of contact with a sick one, or even in contact with a place where the sick worm once had been — like a mulberry leaf — would get sick too.

Pasteur and his assistants continued their experiments. There was still a great deal to learn about the silkworms. By and large, however, the advice Pasteur had given the growers in June 1865, worked. But by the spring of 1867, it was clear this remedy worked only part of the time. Other times, worms with no corpuscles died for no apparent reason. They turned black and squishy and rotted quickly. Pasteur couldn't seem to find any cause for this.

As the weeks passed, his assistants noticed that Pasteur was increasingly uneasy about the mysterious silkworm deaths. One day, wrote one of them, Pasteur "appeared before us almost in tears, and, dropping discouraged into a chair said: 'Nothing is accomplished; there are two diseases!'"

THE SECOND SILKWORM DISEASE

"Two diseases — what excellent news!" one of Pasteur's assistants exclaimed. "Now that we *know* there are two diseases, we can deal with both," another said.

Pasteur brightened. "Let us get back to work," he said.

After further experiments, Pasteur found that the second disease was flacherie; it gave the worms a fatal gassy diarrhea. Earlier investigators had noted the condition, but believed it was part of the pebrine disease. They thought this because many silkworms had both diseases.

Pasteur discovered that silkworms with flacherie had certain kinds of bacteria in their digestive tracts. He immediately told the growers how to find out whether the moths they planned to use for breeding had flacherie.

"First, take several moths from each brood," Pasteur told them. "Remove a small piece of their digestive tracts with the point of a scalpel. Mix this material with a little water and examine it under the microscope. If you see no bacteria, the rest of the brood can be safely bred."

Pasteur also noted that, just like pebrine, flacherie was extremely contagious. He told the growers how to protect the silkworms from infection.

"During hot and humid weather, creased or broken mulberry leaves develop the types of bacteria seen in flacherie. Worms fed on those leaves will get the disease."

He also told them to keep the silkworms' nurseries dry, uncrowded, and well ventilated. "Dampness and crowding weaken the worms' resistance to disease and encourage bacterial growth," he said. "Plenty of fresh air, however, strengthens the worms."

And a regular cleaning of the nursery was a must. Flacherie bacteria lived in spores — tiny sacs in which organisms survive in a kind of hibernation until conditions are just right for them to live again. "Such spores remain in the nursery dust and can cause new outbreaks," he said.

As before, many growers took his advice. Many others decided to wait. Local scientists who were biologists resented Pasteur. It didn't matter that the government had appointed him. So many vicious rumors were spread about him that, in June, Madame Pasteur got a worried letter from her father in which he wrote, "It is being reported here that the failure of Pasteur's process has excited the population of your neighborhood so much that he has had to flee from Alais, pursued by infuriated inhabitants throwing stones at him."

None of this was true, but Pasteur kept very busy proving his theories to everyone.

Pasteur dictating another paper on silkworms to his wife, Marie, at their house at Pont Gisquet, outside the city of Alais (now Alès). (National Library of Medicine.)

In the fall of 1868, after a long, hot summer of silkworm research, Pasteur and his family returned to Paris. Back in their apartment at the Ecole Normale, Pasteur heard what was music to his ears — workmen constructing a new and larger laboratory for him at the order of the Emperor Napoleon III.

With the start of the new school year, Pasteur happily continued his demanding schedule. But on the morning of October 19, he woke up with a tingling in his left side. He thought nothing of it. But during lunch with his family he had a shivering fit. Instead of working, he lay down for a short rest. Then he got ready to go to the Academy of Sciences to read a paper.

"The shivering is gone," he told Marie. Still, she insisted on walking with him for a little distance. When she turned back, she saw Professor Balard, also on his way to the Academy, and asked the elderly scientist to watch over Pasteur. After the session, Pasteur walked back to the Ecole with Balard and another friend. All seemed well. Marie sighed with relief.

That night a tired Pasteur went to bed early. Suddenly, the tingling came back, and worse, he couldn't speak or move. A few minutes later, he could. He cried out to Marie for help. She quickly sent for a doctor. For hours, Pasteur was paralyzed one minute, not paralyzed the next. But by morning, his entire left side was, and remained, paralyzed. He had suffered a severe stroke, just like his mother had so many years ago. He was only 45 years old.

For days, Pasteur hung between life and death. Several

doctors attended him. One prescribed bleeding, and put 16 leeches, blood-sucking worms, behind his ears. Friends took turns sitting with Pasteur through the long nights and dreary days. Many other people paid courtesy visits to inquire about him. A footman from the Emperor and Empress came every morning to get an update on his condition. Almost everyone expected him to die.

But by the end of the week, Pasteur began to improve. One night, he dictated to a student, who was sitting with him, his ideas about a new way to identify silkworm eggs likely to have flacherie. The pupil gave his notes to Jean-Baptiste Dumas the next morning. The amazed and delighted Dumas read them before the Academy of Sciences that very day.

Only one thing bothered the recovering patient. Every day he instructed Marie and Marie Louise to check on the building of his new laboratory. "How are the workmen getting on?" he asked. Every day, they gave him vague answers. Finally Madame Pasteur admitted that the day after Pasteur's stroke, someone ordered the workmen to stop.

Why build a laboratory for a man who is going to die? Pasteur thought bitterly. It made sense. But he hadn't died.

The next time the emperor's aide came to call, Pasteur complained. Shortly afterward, work on the laboratory began again.

Pasteur continued to improve. In January, 1869, he insisted on going back to work. His left side remained slightly paralyzed, leaving him with a limp in his left leg and a stiff left hand. But he was eager to finish his silkworm research. The silkworms had taught him a great deal about the nature of contagious disease. Soon he would begin putting this knowledge to work in investigating other diseases.

How the Infinitely Small is Infinitely Great

Pasteur published a two-volume book on silkworm diseases in 1870. In it, he wrote, "The role of these infinitely small beings [microbes] appears to me to be infinitely great, whether as the cause of different diseases, particularly contagious ones, or by contributing to decomposition and to the return to the atmosphere of everything that has lived." As he began to research animal and then human disease, he often said to new assistants, "Read the studies on the silkworms; it will be ... a good preparation for the investigations that we are about to undertake."

CHAPTER 9

WAR AND THE FIGHT AGAINST KILLER GERMS

"Pasteur, you must not stay in Paris. You will be useless during the siege," said his friend Bertin, the sub-director of the Ecole Normale. Another friend, Dr. Godelier, nodded in agreement.

War with Germany had broken out in July 1870. The French Emperor and nearly his entire army were swiftly defeated and captured. A new French government, a Republic, was quickly formed to continue the war. But now the German army was marching on Paris. French soldiers were setting up barricades to defend the city, and citizens were rushing to join the National Guard.

"I will join the National Guard, like you, Bertin, and fight for my country," said Pasteur.

"My dear friend, you are still half paralyzed from your stroke. They will never accept you," said Dr. Godelier.

"Besides, you cannot even do any research here," added Bertin. The Ecole Normale was empty; the authorities were turning it into a hospital in preparation for the siege. All the students had joined the army and had been sent off to fight. Among them was Pasteur's 18-year-old son, Jean-Baptiste.

Pasteur smiled sadly. "You are right, I will do as you advise," he said.

"You must leave quickly, before the Germans can surround the city," cautioned Dr. Godelier.

Pasteur fled with his family to his home town of Arbois. In this peaceful place, it was hard to believe a war was going on — except when the town crier blew his trumpet to get everyone outside to hear his news. Over the months, this news became worse and worse. The Germans even bombarded Paris, badly damaging the Ecole Normale.

In January 1871, the Pasteurs and the villagers stood outside in the snow to hear the worst news yet. After four months under siege, Paris had surrendered to the German army. The war was over. France had lost.

Everyone was angry and dismayed. "No, it cannot be!" "What will happen to us now?"

"Do you have news of the French army division which is retreating toward Pontarlier?" asked Pasteur anxiously. "My son is with them."

The town crier shrugged. "No news," he said. "Perhaps in a few days."

But the days passed and there was still no news. The Pasteurs grew desperate. They had lost three children to disease. Had they now lost a fourth to war?

"We must go look for him," said Pasteur to Marie. She quickly agreed. Pontarlier, where the army was heading, was just across the mountain from Arbois.

On January 24, Pasteur, Madame Pasteur, and 12-year-old Marie Louise set off in a rickety old horse-drawn carriage, all they could get, across the snow-covered, freezing mountain road. With his bad arm and leg, Pasteur had to leave most of the hard work of getting the carriage through the snow to Madame Pasteur and Marie Louise. At night they slept in drafty little inns along the way. But by the third night they reached Pontarlier.

The town was a terrible sight. Hordes of ragged and exhausted soldiers milled about. Some had built fires in the street to keep themselves warm. Others begged for food or for straw to make a bed.

The anxious family hurried from soldier to soldier, asking about Jean-Baptiste's battalion.

One soldier questioned by Madame Pasteur replied, "All that I can tell you is that out of the 1200 men in that battalion there are but 300 left."

As she frantically began to question someone else, a passing soldier stopped. "You are looking for Sergeant Pasteur? Yes, he is alive. I slept by him last night at Chaffois. He has remained behind because he is ill. You might meet him on the road back to Chaffois."

The Pasteurs stumbled into their old carriage and started back the way they had come. Just outside the town, they saw a battered cart heading toward them. In it, a soldier wrapped up in his overcoat, his hands grasping the edge of the cart, suddenly motioned to them in surprise. It was Jean-Baptiste. He stopped the cart and got out to embrace his family. Everyone was so overwhelmed with emotion that for the moment they could not speak.

Madame Pasteur and Marie Louise returned to Arbois. Pasteur went with Jean-Baptiste to Geneva, where the exhausted and half-starved young man was able to recover his health. He rejoined his regiment in February.

Civil war broke out in Paris in March because of the peace treaty France was forced to sign. It required France

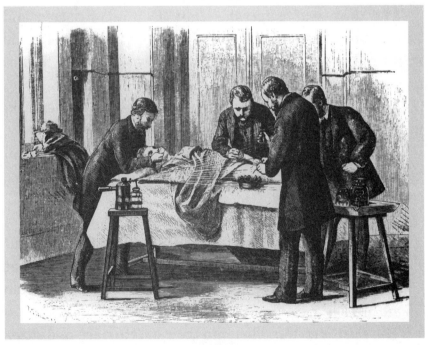

Scottish surgeon Joseph Lister pioneered antiseptic surgery after reading Pasteur's writings. This illustration of the time shows the position of the carbolic spray, towels, and the surgeons. (Corbis / Bettmann.)

to pay Germany such a huge sum of money that France would be bankrupt. The people attacking the government felt the treaty should never have been signed. Pasteur and his family did not return to Paris until September, when order was finally restored.

As he resumed his duties at the Ecole, Pasteur heard with pleasure of the work of Joseph Lister, a Scottish surgeon. Lister had read Pasteur's writings about microbes that caused fermentation and putrefaction. He realized that microbes might also enter a wound during an operation and

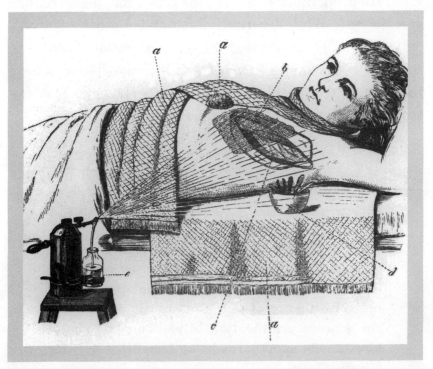

A closer view of how Joseph Lister used carbolic spray to keep a wound purified. He also ordered the towels to be soaked in carbolic solution. (Corbis/Bettmann.)

cause infection. He decided to prevent this by using antiseptics to kill the germs. First, he sterilized all his instruments, sponges and bandages in carbolic acid (the same acid
used on the rabid dog bite wounds of nine-year-old Joseph
Meister). He and his assistants washed their hands in a
solution of it too. During the operation, a carbolic acid
vaporizer sprayed an antiseptic mist around the wound.
Afterwards, before bandaging the wound, Lister swabbed it
with a carbolic acid solution.

Between 1867 and 1869, 34 of 40 Lister patients survived their operations. It was, for that time, an incredible
success rate. While his results astounded other surgeons,
only a few of them adopted his techniques. Most people in
those days, doctors included, found it impossible to believe
that tiny microbes that could only be seen under a microscope had the power to kill people.

Lister Writes Pasteur

**A few years later, in February 1874, Lister wrote
Pasteur thanking him for "having, by your bril-
liant researches, demonstrated to me the truth of
the germ theory of putrefaction... it would...give
you sincere gratification to see at our hospital
how largely mankind is being benefitted by your
labours."**

In the 19th century, people who underwent surgery in hospitals nearly always died, mostly because of widespread unsanitary conditions that let deadly germs spread. Of the 13,000 French soldiers operated on during the recent war, 10,000 died of infection, not their wounds. Near the end of the war, a French doctor, Alphonse Guerin, also read Pasteur's writings on putrefaction. He decided to use antiseptic techniques that were similar to Lister's. He too began to enjoy a high survival rate among his patients.

In 1873, Guerin invited Pasteur, who had recently been elected a member of the Academy of Medicine, to visit his hospital. Pasteur was pleased with Guerin's antiseptic techniques.

"I have only one suggestion," said Pasteur. "Heat your bandages to a very high temperature before using them so all the germs will be killed."

Now that he was a member of the Academy of Medicine, Pasteur visted hospitals more often. As he watched doctors with bloody smocks and dirty hands move down a ward from patient to patient, he realized the patients were being infected by the very people who were supposed to cure them. He began to speak up more at the Academy. In one famous speech, he said, "If I had the honor of being a surgeon...I would use none but perfectly clean instruments...after having cleansed my hands with the greatest care."

But his advice was resented. Many Academy physicians thought Pasteur's Germ Theory of Disease was ridiculous. They also looked down on him as a mere chemist, an interloper elected to the Academy by only one vote. What could he know about medicine anyway? They, the "princes of science" (as doctors were then known) were the experts, not Pasteur.

As usual, Pasteur never gave up. One day a celebrated physician gave a speech at the Academy in which he discussed the epidemics of childbirth fever that were killing so many healthy young women soon after they gave birth. He said the cause was a mystery and might never be found.

Pasteur leaped up from his seat. "The cause is the nursing and medical staff who transport an infectious microbe from a sick woman to a healthy one!" he declared.

The physician, who didn't believe in Pasteur's Germ Theory of Disease, said sneeringly, "Such a microbe will never be found in our lifetime."

Pasteur rushed up to the front of the auditorium. "But it

Pioneers against Childbirth Fever

As early as the 1840s, Dr. Ignace Semmelweiss in Vienna, and Dr. Oliver Wendell Holmes in Boston, both urged the adoption of antiseptic techniques to prevent childbirth fever. Their ideas were derided and ignored, and women continued to die. It was only with the triumph of the Germ Theory of Disease in the late 19th century that the situation began to change.

Islamic Antisepsis

In 10th century Islamic Spain, a Muslim doctor, Al Zahrawi (936 – c.1013) developed a system of using antiseptics to clean wounds. But because of the hostility between Christian Europe and the Islamic World, knowledge of this advance never travelled between the two areas. Not until the 19th century did the idea of antisepsis, the first rule of any medical procedure today, begin to arise in Europe.

has been found," he said, and drew a picture of a microbe shaped like a string of beads on the blackboard.

"There, that is what it looks like!" he said. It was the streptococcus bacterium, well known today even to children who get "strep throat," but in those days something almost no one believed in.

Most of the audience paid no attention to what Pasteur said. But a small and growing group did. They would go on to change the way medicine was practiced.

CHAPTER 10

BEGINNING THE BATTLE AGAINST DEADLY ANTHRAX

"This is how the poor sheep die of anthrax: they tremble, their heads droop helplessly, and they gasp for breath," said a veterinarian friend to Pasteur. "Death comes so quickly that the farmer may not even notice his animals are sick until they fall over and die." The blood of the dead animals clotted and turned coal black, the reason the disease was called anthrax (which means "coal" in Greek).

Determined to prove his Germ Theory of Disease by continuing his fight against diseases, Pasteur had begun research on anthrax in February 1877. Anthrax was like a plague, one so swift and deadly that it killed thousands of farm animals yearly, most of them sheep, in only a few hours. The cost to the farming community was tremendous, not only in France but all over Europe.

Pasteur noted one thing about anthrax right away: it was highly contagious, easily spread from a sick creature to a healthy one. Pasteur had learned a great deal about contagion during his work on silkworm diseases. But anthrax seemed to be super-contagious: the fields where the animals died were considered "cursed" because any other animals grazing there also got sick and died. This happened even when the pastures were not used for years.

But Pasteur heard that sometimes an animal did not get sick in a "cursed" field when others did. No one knew why.

It was certainly a mysterious disease.

Pasteur was not the first scientist to investigate anthrax. Others had been researching it for more than 25 years, with no useful results. And the latest two studies contradicted each other. One scientist claimed that tiny microbes shaped like rods that he saw in the blood and tissues of an anthrax victim caused the disease. Two other scientists injected a rabbit with blood from an anthrax victim. After the rabbit died, they found no rods in its blood. They said that therefore the rods could not cause the disease.

But just in the past year, the great German scientist, Robert Koch, declared he had proved that the rods caused anthrax. In his experiment, he first grew the tiny rods in a nutrient bouillon (a clear organic liquid or soup). He transferred some of the rods to a second bouillon. When these also began to multiply, he transferred a portion of them to a third bouillon. In all, he made eight transfers. He injected a mouse with the eighth bouillon. It died in 24 hours. Under the microscope, Koch found the tiny rods in its spleen. He

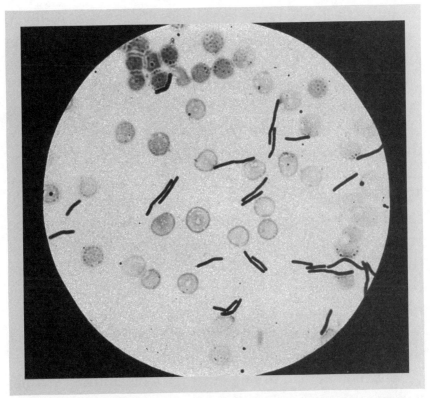

Anthrax rods seen under a microscope. (© Institut Pasteur, Paris.)

felt this was proof that the rod-shaped microbes caused anthrax.

But some scientists said it was possible that something else in the anthrax blood — perhaps something invisible — killed the mouse. They claimed Koch may have transferred this substance along with the blood and the rods from bouillon to bouillon.

This is where Pasteur came in. He decided to begin his research by doing an experiment to doublecheck Koch's results.

Into a flask filled with two ounces of a nutrient bouillon, he inserted one drop of blood full of the tiny rods believed to cause anthrax. When the rods began to multiply in the bouillon, he took a single drop of liquid from the flask, and put it into a second flask, which also contained two ounces of bouillon. He repeated this procedure 100 times. By now, the original drop of blood had been so greatly diluted — mathematically speaking, of the order of 1 part in 100 to the 100th power — that not even a molecule of it was left. Only the rods were left, descendants of the original rods in the one drop of blood — because they kept growing in each of the 100 bouillons.

Pasteur injected liquid from the 100th flask into several rabbits and guinea pigs. They all died. Under the microscope, he saw the rods in their blood. Here was definite proof that the rods alone had killed the animals.

But now, he had to find out why some anthrax victims had no anthrax rods in their blood.

In June, Pasteur travelled to Chartres to examine three animals that died of anthrax. A veterinarian friend there, Dr. Boutet, chose them according to Pasteur's instructions.

The first animal was a sheep that had been dead about 16 hours. Pasteur found its blood was full of anthrax rods.

The second animal, a horse dead 24 hours, had rods in its blood, but also a long, very thin, transparent microbe. Aha! thought Pasteur. He knew this microbe; he discovered it a year ago during his fermentation studies. He had named it the septic vibrio. It caused decay (putrefaction).

In the blood of the third victim, a cow dead for more than

two days, Pasteur found a great many septic vibrios, but only a few anthrax rods.

Then Pasteur did an experiment. He injected the sheep blood full of the rods into a guinea pig. When the guinea pig died, he found that its blood was also full of the rods. He injected a second guinea pig with blood from the horse, and a third with blood from the cow. After they died, he found that their blood contained no rods.

Now he knew why some anthrax victims had no rods in their blood.

Pasteur presented his findings to both the Academy of Sciences and the Academy of Medicine.

"The longer an anthrax victim has been dead, the fewer anthrax rods will be found in its blood," he said. The anthrax bacteria multiplied only until the creature died. Then they began to disappear from the blood stream. Once enough time passed, an anthrax victim would have no rods in its blood at all.

As for the septic vibrio, he continued, "It normally inhabits the intestines of both living humans and animals, in very small numbers, and without causing any harm. But at death, the septic vibrio invades the blood stream, multiplying rapidly as it begins to cause the dead body to decay."

But, he added, once the harmless septic vibrio left the intestines and got into the blood stream to start its work of making the dead body decay, it turned into something very dangerous. An injection of blood filled with it would kill an animal of blood poisoning — septicemia. The guinea pigs

Accepting the Germ Theory of Disease

Many people, not just doctors, found it hard to believe in the Germ Theory of Disease. The idea that tiny organisms invisible to the naked eye could harm much larger creatures such as humans and animals went against basic common sense. Doctors also resisted believing the theory because it meant that they infected their own patients with their unsanitary practices. Pasteur had to keep proving his theory over and over until finally one day it replaced the old way of looking at disease and became the model on which today's medicine is based.

A historian named Thomas Kuhn described this kind of change in thinking as a "paradigm shift" (pronounced: para-dime). Such a shift always opens up many new possibilities because the world is now seen in a different

injected with blood from the horse and cow died from this, not from anthrax. "Septicemia," said Pasteur, "is a putrefaction of the living organism."

Pasteur had now proved *twice* that the tiny rods in an anthrax victim's blood were the cause of anthrax — the first time by improving on Robert Koch's experiment, and the second time by proving that the reason some animals that died of anthrax had no rods, or only a few rods, in their blood was because the rods began to disappear from the bloodstream after death.

way. But it often takes a long time for a paradigm shift to happen. For instance, in Europe, it took people many years to believe that the Earth was round instead of flat. But once people no longer feared they might fall off the edge of the world, they decided to travel around it, and as a result they discovered new lands and civilizations.

Another paradigm shift was beginning to occur in regard to the role of women in medicine and science. In 1849, in the United States, Elizabeth Blackwell graduated from medical school to become the first woman doctor of modern times. In 1877, when Pasteur began his research on anthrax, Marie Curie, who would be the first woman to win a Nobel prize in science, was 10 years old.

Pasteur then set out to answer another question: why did the septic vibrio grow after death while the anthrax microbes began to disappear?

He found that, like the butryric acid fermentation he discovered 16 years earlier, the septic vibrio grew only in the absence of air, that is, it was *anaerobic*. But the anthrax microbe needed air to live, that is, it was *aerobic*. Since at death, the body no longer breathed in any air, the anthrax rods began to die out. The anaerobic septic vibrios, on the other hand, now had the perfect environment in which to grow.

Despite Pasteur's dazzling proofs of the Germ Theory of Disease in the case of anthrax, many physicians and veterinarians continued to oppose his ideas about specific germs causing specific diseases. They regarded him as an arrogant, wrong-headed chemist whose lack of medical training led him up the wrong tree. As one opponent put it: "Applied to chronic diseases, these doctrines condemn us to the research of specific remedies...and all progress is arrested.... Specificity immobilizes medicine."

As usual, Pasteur was not discouraged. He and his assistants plugged away at their research, making weekly trips to Chartres where they had set up a laboratory. Finding the cause of a disease was only the first step. Finding a way to prevent it was something else again. Pasteur was sure he would conquer anthrax sooner or later. Right now, it looked as if it would be later. Maybe much later.

11

CAN PASTEUR FIND THE RIGHT WEAPON AGAINST ANTHRAX?

One day at a farm outside Chartres, Pasteur and his assistants, Emile Roux and Charles Chamberland, were walking with a local farmer and discussing animals that had died of anthrax. Suddenly, Pasteur stopped and pointed at a field next to them.

"Why is the earth a different color over there?" he asked.

The farmer, Monsieur Maunoury, replied, "I buried several sheep that died of anthrax there last year."

Pasteur went up to the fence and looked at the field for a long time. So long that the farmer began to get impatient. But he didn't want to interrupt this scientist who was trying to help. Roux and Chamberland, of course, were used to Pasteur concentrating like this.

As Pasteur gazed at the section of the field where the earth was a different color, he noticed that it had many tiny mounds scattered about the surface. He knew these were the kinds of mounds that earthworms made as they tunnelled up out of the ground.

"I believe the earthworms are bringing anthrax spores from those dead animals up with them," said Pasteur.

Pasteur was familiar with spores from his work on silkworm diseases. Spores were microbes encased in a protective sac in which they existed in a kind of hibernation. This way the microbes could last for years and, when conditions were right — for instance, when a sheep began to graze in the field — they could suddenly come back to life and cause disease again.

Pasteur went into the field and carefully collected some earthworms. As his assistant Roux put it, "Pasteur never stopped at ideas, but immediately proceeded to the experiment... The earth extracted from the intestine of one of the worms, injected into guinea pigs, forthwith gave them anthrax."

Pasteur hurried to tell Monsieur Maunoury and all the other farmers not to bury any animals that died of anthrax in their pastures, but instead to burn the bodies or else bury them "in sandy or chalky soils, poor, dry, and unsuitable to the life of earthworms." That way, there would be no more "cursed fields" in which grazing animals got anthrax.

This advice was a great help to the farmers. However, Pasteur wanted to find out how to prevent anthrax altogether. But while his and his assistants' experiments were many, progress was slow.

As part of his research, Pasteur studied the writings of Edward Jenner, an English doctor who protected people from deadly smallpox some 80 years before by injecting them with material from a cowpox sore. Cowpox was a mild disease of cattle that milkmaids often got. When a milkmaid told Jenner that people who got cowpox never got smallpox, Jenner figured out that cowpox had to be smallpox in a much milder form. He also realized that the person who recovered from cowpox was immune to, that is, protected from, the nearly always fatal smallpox. Jenner called his cowpox injection "vaccination," from the Latin *vaccinus,* meaning cow.

Pasteur thought about the few sheep that did not get anthrax in a "cursed" field when other sheep did. He wondered if these sheep had gotten a mild form of the disease,

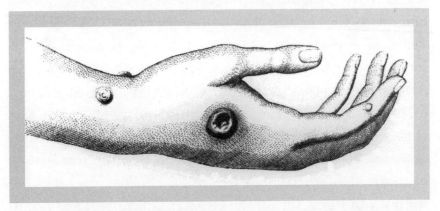

Jenner's cowpox inoculation against smallpox: Pus from this cowpox lesion [sore] was used by Jenner to perform a successful smallpox vaccination on May 14, 1798. (Corbis/Bettmann.)

recovered from it, and were then immune — just like the milkmaids who got cowpox and were immune from smallpox. Maybe there was a way to make a weak anthrax solution — a vaccination, or vaccine — that would protect sheep and other animals from anthrax.

But Pasteur wasn't the first scientist to think this way. Others had followed Jenner's lead, trying to protect animals — and even humans — by injecting them with mild doses of diseases. None of these attempts worked, and worse, often the "mild dose" was enough to cause the full-blown disease.

Nothing seemed to be working for Pasteur and his assistants either. It was very frustrating. But they continued to press on.

One day, Pasteur had a welcome interruption: a professor from the Toulouse Veterinary School asked him to find a nutrient bouillon to grow some chicken cholera germs he had isolated. After many tries, Pasteur developed the right bouillon to grow (culture) the germs. When he injected some hens with the culture, they all quickly died. He set up a series of experiments with the cultures, but before they could be carried out, he and Madame Pasteur went to Arbois, leaving the chicken cholera project in the care of two assistants. The Pasteurs' daughter Marie Louise was engaged, and the happy parents were busy with preparations for the wedding. Their son, Jean-Baptise, was also to be married later that year.

Back in Paris, one of the assistants, Emile Roux, decided to try an experiment of his own. He began by allowing a flask of the chicken cholera culture to be exposed to the air.

His idea was that doing this might make the culture weaker. Weeks later, he injected some hens with this exposed culture. None of the hens died, though some got sick. After the sick hens recovered, he injected all the hens with a fresh and virulent (deadly) culture. Almost all of the hens survived. Roux was delighted. This had to be the way they could develop a chicken cholera vaccine!

When Pasteur returned, Roux told him about his experiments and the results. The amazed Pasteur thought for a few minutes, then exclaimed excitedly, "That is it, the surviving chickens were made *immune* by being *vaccinated!*" Then he and Roux and the rest of the assistants got to work to develop just the right vaccine culture, one weak enough to give chickens only a slight case of cholera (and without killing them), but strong enough to protect them in the future from the full disease. Pasteur named Roux's process of weakening the deadly culture in the air "attenuation." He hoped to use this same process to develop a vaccine for anthrax — and perhaps for other diseases too.

In February 1880, Pasteur reported the development of the successful chicken cholera vaccine to both the Academy of Sciences and the Academy of Medicine. But his imagination was already eagerly leaping far ahead of animal diseases to human ones. He ended by saying that "as a result of the facts I have presented," research could now begin on vaccines for "the virulent diseases that have so many times devastated and still devastate humanity."

But first he still had to conquer anthrax.

THE GREAT ANTHRAX VACCINE TRIAL

Pasteur quickly got back to work on anthrax.

"We will use the same method on anthrax germs that worked on the chicken cholera germs," he told his staff. "I will grow them in a nutrient bouillon and then expose them to the air to weaken them."

It didn't work.

When he put anthrax germs into a nutrient bouillon, they turned into spores. This was very discouraging. Pasteur knew from his earlier research that spores could live in a kind of hibernation state for years without food or water and, perhaps more important, they were not weakened by being exposed to air. When they came back to life, they were just as deadly.

Later that evening, after Marie, as usual, read the newspaper to him out loud, he told her of the setback. He seemed dejected.

"You will find another way," Marie said.

"How do you know that?" he asked a little grumpily.

"Because you always do," she replied cheerfully.

She was right. After several months of experiments, Pasteur finally found out how to keep the anthrax germs in the nutrient bouillon from changing into spores: he heated them to 42 degrees Centigrade (107.6 degrees Fahrenheit). Then he exposed them to the air. In a week, the germs became weak, just as the chicken cholera germs had. Now he could develop a vaccine!

After some trial and error, Pasteur figured out a two-step process for a vaccine. First, he injected some sheep with a very weak anthrax culture. Twelve days later, he injected them with a stronger one. After two weeks, he tested the vaccinated sheep by injecting them with a full strength culture. The sheep stayed healthy. Then he injected some unvaccinated sheep with the same full strength culture. They quickly died.

The anthrax vaccine worked!

But he didn't stop there.

"Let us see what will happen if we let some of the weakened anthrax germs develop into spores," he said to his assistants. The resulting spores were as weak as the germs they developed from. Pasteur immediately realized that using weakened spores for the vaccine was more efficient because spores were more easily transported and stored than germs.

On February 28, 1881, before the Academy of Sciences, Pasteur caused a sensation when he announced the development of the successful anthrax vaccine, as well as his hopes for soon being able "to apply it on a large scale" outside the laboratory to prove its effectiveness.

A veterinary surgeon, Monsieur Rossignol, quickly offered Pasteur the opportunity for a large field trial on his own farm in the small town of Pouilly le Fort, near the city of Melun, about 25 miles southeast of Paris. The eager Rossignol speedily collected money from interested parties to pay for the trial and even persuaded the Melun Agricultural Society to oversee it.

But Rossignol was no friend of Pasteur or the Germ Theory of Disease. He expected the trial to fail and Pasteur to be disgraced. Only a month before Pasteur made his announcement, Rossignol had published an article in the *Veterinary Press*, in which he sarcastically wrote:

"Microbiolatry is the fashion, it reigns undisputed; it is a doctrine which must not even be discussed, especially when its Pontiff, the learned M. Pasteur, has pronounced the sacramental words, *I have spoken*.... henceforth the germ theory must have precedence... the Microbe alone is true, and Pasteur is its prophet."

Pasteur knew that many doctors and veterinarians wanted him to fail, for his Germ Theory of Disease to be proven wrong. But he was confident this would not happen.

He told his assistants, "What has succeeded in the laboratory on fourteen sheep will succeed just as well at Melun on fifty."

In the trial, half the sheep would be vaccinated, and half would not. Then both groups would be given a full dose of the anthrax germ. Besides the sheep, some cows, an ox, and a goat were added to the trial because anthrax also affected other farm animals.

Pasteur was undisturbed. "Be sure not to make a mistake in the bottles," he said jokingly as he and his assistants left the laboratory on May 5 to give the group of animals to be vaccinated their first injection.

A surprise awaited them at Pouilly le Fort. Rossignol had been so busy spreading the word about the anthrax trial that when Pasteur and his assistants arrived, they found a huge crowd eagerly watching their every move. Among the spectators was the Paris correspondent of *The*

Raging Opposition

Sometimes it seemed as if every physician and veterinarian took great pains to oppose Pasteur. So much so, that the *Journal de la Médecine et de la Chimie* felt compelled to defend him: "He is not a medical man, and yet, guided by his genius, he opens new paths across the most arduous studies of medical science. Instead of being offered the tribute of attention and admiration which he deserves, he meets with a raging opposition from some quarrelsome individuals, ever inclined to contradict after listening as little as possible."

Sheep being inoculated against anthrax. (© Institut Pasteur, Paris.)

Times of London. Rossignol was overjoyed: now, he was sure, Pasteur would be *internationally* disgraced!

On May 5, twenty-five sheep, five cows, and one ox were vaccinated. Pasteur's assistants remained in Pouilly le Fort to check on the animals every day. After 12 days, they gave the animals the second, stronger injection.

Then on May 31, before an even greater crowd, both the vaccinated and the unvaccinated animals (twenty-four sheep, one goat, and four cows) were injected with a full dose of the deadly anthrax germs.

Everyone would come back to see the results on June 2.

On June 1, Pasteur's assistants returned to Paris and told him that several of the vaccinated sheep had fevers. Then a telegram arrived from Rossignol saying that one vaccinated sheep was ill and perhaps dying.

According to his assistant Roux, Pasteur's "faith was shaken, as though he feared that the experimental method might betray him."

Pasteur even accused Roux of having spoiled the field trial.

"You must have been careless with the vaccine!" he exclaimed. Madame Pasteur tried to calm Pasteur, telling him that they had to get up early the next morning to get to Pouilly le Fort. But Pasteur still spent an anxious and sleepless night.

The next morning at 8 o'clock, a telegram arrived from Rossignol saying the sick sheep was well. He added that 18 of the unvaccinated animals were dead, and the others were dying; but all the vaccinated animals were healthy. Rossignol ended his message with the words "stunning success."

An elated Pasteur returned in triumph to Pouilly le Fort with his family, and some friends and dignitaries. When they got off the train, an enthusiastic crowd welcomed them. Pasteur, full of confidence again, stood up in the carriage that was to carry them to the farm and exclaimed to the crowd: "Well then! Men of little faith!"

When they reached the farm, a great cheer rose from the waiting crowd. All the vaccinated animals were healthy. Of the poor unvaccinated animals, 21 sheep and the one goat were dead, and two sheep were dying. The four cows were sick, but would eventually recover.

It was as clear as could be that the vaccine worked.

Reporters clamored for interviews. Local farmers and members of agricultural, veterinary, and medical societies crowded around to congratulate Pasteur. Perhaps no congratulation was so welcome as that of Rossignol.

"I was wrong," he told Pasteur. From then on, Rossignol was a fervent advocate of the Germ Theory of Disease.

News of Pasteur's astonishing success spread throughout Europe. And it seemed that every farmer in Europe wanted the new anthrax vaccine.

CHAPTER 13

TACKLING RABIES: THE MOST VICIOUS KILLER

Pasteur began research on rabies while he was still working on the anthrax vaccine. One blustery December afternoon in 1880, he and two assistants hurried to the Hospital of Sainte-Eugénie. Pasteur's friend Dr. Lannelongue had sent him a message that a five-year-old boy with rabies had just been admitted. The child had been bitten on the face a month before.

"The boy is in the last stages," said Dr. Lannelongue. "It is hopeless for him, but perhaps you may find some way to help others."

But Pasteur, the loving father who lost three of his own children to disease, found it unbearable to see the little boy going into spasms, crying for water but unable to swallow it, and screaming with mindless rage.

"We cannot stay," he murmured to Dr. Lannelongue. He and his assistants walked over to say a sad farewell to the boy's parents and left.

The child died the next morning. Pasteur returned to the hospital and took some saliva (mucus) samples from the dead boy's mouth. Pasteur never forgot the horror of what happened back in Arbois when he was only eight years old: the rabid wolf that bit so many farmers, and how all but one of them died. How afraid he had been that he too could be bitten! But he had never seen in person how horrible such a death could be.

Pasteur had wanted to use his Germ Theory to fight human diseases for a long time. But he could not experiment on people to produce a vaccine. He needed to work on a disease that attacked both humans and animals. That disease, he decided, would be rabies.

If he could make a rabies vaccine to save animals, perhaps it could lead to a rabies vaccine for humans, too. And once one human vaccine was developed, vaccines could be developed for other diseases, perhaps even the ones that had killed his three children.

Back in his laboratory, he mixed the dead boy's mucus with water, then injected two rabbits with the liquid. Both died in a day and a half. He went on with his experiments but after several weeks he realized the microbe in the boy's mucus was not the rabies microbe.

As he explained to Marie over dinner, "First, the rabbits

died too quickly. Rabies has a long incubation period." It took weeks, sometimes even months, before an infected person (or animal) showed any symptoms.

"Second, the rabbits that died never had any rabies symptoms," he went on. He added that he had found the same microbe in the saliva of children who died from other diseases, and even in a healthy grown up.

"I have to find another way," he said. "Again."

Pasteur tried using saliva, and even blood, from rabid dogs. But these experiments did not produce any good results either. Nor could he see anything that might be the rabies microbe under the microscope.

Where was *the microbe that caused rabies?* he wondered.

After mulling over the problem for some time, he realized the reason he could not find the microbe had to be because it was too small to see with the microscopes of that time.

But what was he going to do now? He needed to grow the rabies microbe in order to come up with a vaccine.

"Why don't we try to grow the microbe by inserting brain tissue from a dog that died of rabies into the brain of a healthy dog?" suggested his assistant Emile Roux. Since rabies attacked the nervous system — primarily the brain and spine — this procedure might produce rabies in a short period of time.

It did. The healthy dog got rabies symptoms in two weeks.

Then Pasteur and his assistants found that this method of growing the "invisible" rabies microbe worked in rabbits too — and, in rabbits, the symptoms appeared in only six days. But now that they were able to grow the microbe, how were they going to develop a vaccine?

Precisely because rabies attacked the nervous system, Pasteur decided to experiment with the spinal cords of rabbits that died of the disease. (The nervous system uses the spinal cord to send messages from the brain to the body.) He ground up some spinal cords and made a solution out of them with a little water. When he injected other rabbits with the liquid, they got rabies. Pasteur was elated. He could use the spinal cords to develop a vaccine!

"Seeing" the Rabies Microbe

Pasteur was right in his guess that the rabies microbe was too small to be seen. That was because this microbe was a virus, an organism very different from and much tinier than the bacteria microbes Pasteur did see with his microscope. Scientists first saw the rabies virus only after the electron microscope was invented in 1930. One thing Pasteur did not guess was that viruses, unlike bacteria microbes, could not grow in a nutrient bouillon, but only in the body of a living creature. But by using living animals to grow the virus, Pasteur unknowingly did the right thing.

But the cords were too virulent (deadly) to leave out in the air to "attenuate" or weaken, so that a vaccine could be made of them. How would they get around this problem?

One day Pasteur came across an experiment his assistant Roux was doing. Roux had wanted to know how long a rabid spinal cord would stay rabid. So he invented a flask with two openings, one on top and one on the side near the bottom. Both openings were closed with a wad of cotton, and a cord was hung from the wad that closed the top opening. The cotton kept out dust and germs, but air could get in to "attenuate" the cord.

"At the sight of this flask, Pasteur became so absorbed in his thoughts that I did not dare disturb him," wrote Pasteur's nephew, Adrien Loir, who also worked in the laboratory. Pasteur looked at the flask for a very long time. Then he told Loir to order similar flasks for him from the glass blower.

As Loir wrote years later, "The sight of Roux's flasks had given him the idea of keeping the spinal cord in a container with caustic potash to prevent putrefaction, and allowing the penetration of oxygen to attenuate the virus."

Once they were able to weaken the spinal cords, Pasteur and his assistants began to experiment with injecting these ground up spinal cords into dogs. They found that injections of cords from rabbits dead only a day always produced rabies. Injections of two-week-old cords caused no illness.

Through trial and error, Pasteur developed a series of 14 injections, one given each day, starting with a two-week-old cord, then a 13-day-old cord, and so on until, on the last day, a rabid cord from a freshly killed rabbit was used.

A portrait of Pasteur looking at a rabid rabbit spine in the specially designed flask. (National Library of Medicine.)

After several dogs were given this series of 14 vaccinations, Pasteur decided to test them. He inserted rabies tissue into the brains of some of these dogs. He let rabid dogs

Pasteur on Animal Experimentation

His son-in-law and biographer, Rene Valery-Radot wrote: "Pasteur had a great horror of useless sufferings, and always insisted on anesthesia [for the animals]." According to Emile Roux, "Pasteur felt a veritable repugnance toward [animal experimentation].... He was present without too much squeamishness at simple operations, such as a subcutaneous inoculation [injection], and yet, if the animal cried a little, he immediately felt pity and lavished on the victim consolation and encouragement which would have been comical had it not been touching."

Today there is a great deal of debate on whether and/or how much animal experimentation is necessary. Many people claim that it is the only way to fight disease. Many others feel it is unethical and that other ways can be found to do medical research.

bite the other vaccinated dogs. All the vaccinated dogs remained healthy. The vaccine worked!

Pasteur then decided to find out if an unvaccinated dog could be saved after it was bitten. His theory was that because rabies' incubation period (the time it takes for symptoms to appear) was so long, that the 14-

day series of vaccinations might stop the disease from developing.

He put two healthy dogs in a pen with a rabid one. The rabid dog bit them both. One bitten dog was given the series of injections, the other was not. The vaccinated dog did not get rabies; the unvaccinated one did. Pasteur now knew that he was on the way to developing a vaccine that some day could be used on humans who had been bitten by rabid animals — people like Nicole, the farmer who had been bitten in Pasteur's home town so long ago.

By the summer of 1884, news of Pasteur's successful work on a rabies vaccine for dogs had spread. People bitten by rabid animals wrote begging him to treat them. Pasteur refused. He wrote to one person that "My research is not yet at the point which would permit me to act on man."

The next spring, Pasteur moved most of his experimental animals into a new laboratory, a renovated barn on the outskirts of Paris. By now he was so confident about his vaccine that he wrote his childhood friend, Jules Vercel, "I am much inclined to begin on myself — inoculating myself with rabies, and then arresting the consequences." He continued to turn down pleas to vaccinate other people.

Then on July 6, 1885, the badly bitten, terrified nine-year-old Joseph Meister, his desperate mother and their neighbor, appeared at his laboratory door.

It was fairly easy to say "no" to letters asking for help. It was quite different to come face to face with an actual child who was certain to die of his many terrible bite wounds.

14

WHAT HAPPENED WITH THE RABIES VACCINE

"This is your last inoculation, Joseph," said Pasteur, walking into the boy's room with Dr. Grancher. It was July 16, 1885 and the last inoculation was a serum made of the rabid spinal cord of a rabbit that died the day before.

The little boy was tired from playing and running around all day. As Pasteur watched, Joseph cheerfully let Dr. Grancher give him the injection in his stomach and went peacefully to sleep.

Pasteur did not sleep a wink. He was terrified that this injection, the most deadly one of all, would kill Joseph.

It didn't. Joseph woke up happy and ready to play.

But this was only the first day, thought Pasteur. Perhaps Joseph would develop symptoms later on.

But now that Joseph's treatment was finished, Madame Pasteur got Pasteur to spend a few days of rest in the country with their daughter and son-in-law. Each day Pasteur received a telegram from Dr. Grancher about Joseph's condition. Each day he feared the telegram would bring bad news. But Joseph remained healthy, and returned home with his mother on July 27.

Pasteur began to relax — but only a little. He sent Joseph a package of stamped envelopes and asked him to write him once a week and say how he was. Joseph stayed well. On August 3, Pasteur wrote his son, Jean-Baptiste: "Very good news last night of the bitten lad.... It will be thirty-one days tomorrow since he was bitten."

During the rest of the summer, which, as usual, the Pasteurs spent in Arbois, Pasteur continued to get updates on Joseph. The boy showed no signs of rabies. Pasteur's vaccine for dogs had saved the life of a human being.

On October 26, 1885, Pasteur caused a sensation when he reported on Joseph's successful rabies treatment before the Academy of Sciences.

Then Pasteur dropped another bombshell: he was, at this very moment, treating another rabies victim, Jean-Baptiste Jupille, a fourteen year-old shepherd boy.

Jupille and six younger boys had been watching over their sheep when suddenly a mad dog came up from the road and attacked them. They ran away, but Jupille turned back to fight the dog so the smaller boys could make their escape. He was severely bitten on both arms before managing to kill the dog.

The Mayor of Villers-Farlay, Jupille's home town, had visited Pasteur in nearby Arbois during the past summer. He wrote Pasteur begging him to treat this heroic boy. Pasteur's answer was an immediate yes. This time he had every confidence that he could save someone.

After Pasteur made his stunning announcement, a member of the Academy recommended Jupille for a prize. All the other speakers leaped up to praise Pasteur. One was H. Bouley, the chairman of the Academy, who said, "...the date of the present meeting will remain forever memorable in the history of medicine... [because of] the discovery of an efficacious means of preventive treatment for a disease, the incurable nature of which was a legacy handed down by one century to another. From this day, humanity is armed with a means of fighting the fatal disease of hydrophobia and of preventing its onset. It is to Monsieur Pasteur that we owe this..."

Most of the medical and scientific community was enthusiastic about Pasteur's discovery. But some were horrified. One physician was overheard to say, in private, "Yes, Pasteur is an assassin!"

The final vote, however, was with the public. And their response was overwhelmingly positive. Pasteur was already famous for his anthrax vaccine. But now, because of the rabies vaccine, his fame spread rapidly throughout the entire world. Bitten victims began to stream to his laboratory from all over.

Then Pasteur had a tragic failure. On November 9, ten-year-old Louise Pelletier was brought to him. She had been bitten on the head 37 days before, and the wound was still unhealed and full of pus. Pasteur knew her case was hopeless. But he could not say no to her desperate parents.

At first, the treatment seemed to work. Louise returned to school. But then she grew sick. New inoculations were tried. Nothing worked. Pasteur was by her bedside with her parents when the girl died on December 2.

"I did so wish I could have saved your little one," he said to the parents. As he left and went down the stairs, tears streamed down his face.

Pasteur's enemies jumped on his failure. As Dr. Grancher reported: "Certain political and medical journals... conducted a violent campaign against Pasteur. Even in the colleges of

What Louise's Father, Monsieur Pelletier, Wrote about Pasteur a Few Years Later

"Among great men whose life I am acquainted with... I do not see any other capable of sacrificing...long years of work, of endangering a great fame, and of acceping willingly a painful failure, simply for humanity's sake."

Paris, students would split into Pasteurians and anti-Pasteurians and engage in fights."

But the rabies victims continued to arrive, to be treated, and to survive.

Four bitten American children from working-class families were sent to Paris with money raised by the *New York Herald*. All were saved.

On March 1, 1886, Pasteur reported to the Academy of Sciences that of 350 people treated for rabies, only one died. But because the increasing numbers of people arriving for treatment overwhelmed his laboratory, he asked the Academy to set up a special clinic to handle these patients.

The Academy proposed that the clinic be part of a larger facility to be called the Pasteur Institute, which would also research other diseases.

Nineteenth century engraving of the original Pasteur Institute in Paris. (© Institut Pasteur, Paris.)

Pasteur's seventieth birthday celebration at the Sorbonne University. (National Library of Medicine.)

At long last, Pasteur had triumphed; the Germ Theory of Disease had been accepted, and now with the Institute, major efforts would be made to conquer other diseases. All that was needed now was the money to build it.

Then Pasteur faced his greatest challenge yet — nineteen badly-bitten Russian peasants arrived, five of them so sick that they had to be carried by stretcher to the Hotel Dieu Hospital. The men had been attacked more than two weeks earlier. The only French they knew was "Pasteur," which they kept repeating.

All of Paris was agog. Could Pasteur save any of them?

He saved 16 of the 19. The news was flashed far and wide. Pasteur's enemies talked only of the three Russians who died, but the Russian Tsar sent his brother, the Grand

Duke Vladimir, to award Pasteur a medal, the diamond cross of the Order of Saint Anne of Russia. The Tsar also donated 100,000 francs to help build the Pasteur Institute.

Contributions for the Institute began to pour in from all over the world. On November 14, 1888, the Pasteur Institute was dedicated by the President of France. Honors continued to be heaped on Pasteur, including a huge government-sponsored celebration with hundreds of dignitaries in 1892 to mark his 70th birthday. By now, Pasteur

The Pasteur Institute

One of the greatest medical research facilities in the world, the Pasteur Institute today has branches in many countries. Pasteur's former assistant, Emile Roux, became a renowned scientist in his own right here. It was at the Pasteur Institute that, in 1983, Luc Montagnier and his team discovered the AIDS virus. (In the United States, the virus was rediscovered a little later by Robert Gallo and his team at the National Institutes of Health. Both teams are searching for a vaccine.

From an original staff of 15, the Pasteur Institute has grown to more than 2,800 in the Paris headquarters alone, 1,100 of whom are scientists. Scientists at the Institute have won 8 Nobel Prizes.

was frail and sickly. But at this birthday celebration he finally met one of his greatest admirers, Dr. Joseph Lister, who had pioneered the use of antiseptic techniques after reading Pasteur's writings.

Pasteur had become France's greatest national hero. Although he oversaw the Pasteur Institute, he could no longer work as before because of his ill health. He spent most of his time with his family, especially his two grand-children, Camille and Louis Pasteur Vallery-Radot. He died peacefully in bed on September 28, 1895.

All of France was plunged into mourning. A state funeral was held on October 5, with a church service at the Cathedral of Notre Dame. Pasteur was buried at the Pasteur Institute in a beautiful chapel decorated with mosaics that depicted his major discoveries and accomplishments.

CONTINUING WHAT LOUIS PASTEUR STARTED

By establishing the Germ Theory of Disease and by successfully developing vaccines against anthrax and rabies, Louis Pasteur threw open the door for future scientists to conquer other diseases.

Among the ones medical science found vaccines for were diptheria, cholera, bubonic plague, malaria, tetanus, whooping cough, measles (rubeola), German measles (rubella), mumps, influenza, hepatitis B, tuberculosis, typhoid, typhus, and yellow fever. (Today, scientists have more than 30 different modern vaccines for rabies alone.) In the 1960s, the Salk and Sabine vaccines for polio, a crippling disease that most often struck young children, all but eliminated the disease. Between 1965 and 1977, the World Health Organization, an arm of the United Nations, led the successful effort to eliminate dreaded smallpox all throughout the world.

In spite of these successes, the battle against disease is never totally won. Poorer Third World countries often cannot afford adequate medical care for their citizens, and many "conquered" diseases are rampant. To scientists' dismay, conquered diseases also develop strains resistant to current treatments, and new ones must be found. And deadly new diseases suddenly crop up. The spread of diseases is helped by the fact that today there is so much international travel. Germs travel along with people.

The AIDS epidemic, which sprang up in the early 1980s, causes millions of deaths worldwide every year. As yet, there is no effective vaccine. In the American Southwest, in 1993, an outbreak of hantavirus, a flu-like respiratory disease (first discovered near the Hantaan River in Korea), quickly killed 16 people. In Zaire (now Congo) in 1995, the Ebola virus (named for a nearby river) caused terrible symptoms such as bodily bleeding as it quickly killed its victims. There is no vaccine or effective treatment for either of these.

To continue what Pasteur started, to fight the ongoing battle against disease, the world constantly needs young people who are interested in medical science to become its new scientists, doctors, researchers, technicians, experimenters, and administrators.

Will you be one of them?

TIMELINES

The World During Louis Pasteur's Life

The nineteenth century was the heyday of the Industrial Revolution in Europe and America; it was made possible by inventions too numerous to be all listed here. During this time European countries also made many areas (and even countries) in Asia, Africa, and South America into their colonies or protectorates.

1820s–1840s   Michael Faraday, a British chemist and physicist, paves the way for the Industrial Revolution with many important discoveries about electrical processes, electromagnetism, and chemicals.

1829   First steam locomotive runs in U.S.

1832   Samuel Morse invents the telegraph

1834   Slavery is abolished in the British Empire.

1837   The 18-year-old Victoria becomes Queen of England, and inaugurates the Victorian Age.

1839-1842   The Opium war breaks out when China tries to prevent Britain from selling Indian opium to the Chinese. Britain wins.

1841   James Ross discovers the continent of Antarctica.

1844   A dentist, William Morton, first uses ether as an anesthetic.

1846–onward A potato blight in Ireland causes more than one million starvation deaths; millions of survivors emigrate, most of them to America.

1848   Revolts break out in many European countries as people demand more rights. On September 7, Austria abolishes serfdom. (France abolished it in 1789, Prussia (Germany) in 1807.) In France, the

	King abdicates and a Republic is proclaimed. On December 10, Louis Napoleon, a nephew of Napoleon Bonaparte, is elected President.
1852	Louis Napoleon establishes the Second French Empire with himself as Emperor.
1854	Commodore Perry of the U.S. Navy sails into Tokyo harbor and forces a trade treaty on Japan.
1859	Charles Darwin causes a sensation when he publishes *The Origin of Species,* his book on the theory of human evolution.
1861	On March 3, Russian serfs are freed. In the United States, the Civil War breaks out after Abraham Lincoln is elected President and the southern, slave-owning states secede from the Union.
1862	Lincoln declares all slaves free as of January 1, 1863.
1865	The Civil War is won by the Union side. Lincoln is assassinated.
1870	The Franco-Prussian war breaks out; the French emperor's army is defeated. A revolt in Paris establishes a Republic, which carries on the war.
1871	France is defeated and has to pay heavy reparations.
1876	Alexander Graham Bell invents the telephone; Thomas Alva Edison invents the phonograph.
1887	France organizes its territories in Southeast Asia (present-day Vietnam and Cambodia) into one unit, named Union Indo-Chinoise.
1888	George Eastman develops the Kodak box camera. Serfdom is abolished in Brazil.
1895	G. Marconi invents the wireless telegraph; W. Roentgen discovers X-rays.

Louis Pasteur's Life

1822	Pasteur is born on December 27 in the village of Dôle.
1827	The Pasteur family moves to Arbois.
1843	Pasteur enters the Ecole Normale Supérieure.
1848	Pasteur makes his famous discovery about the paratartrate acid crystals.
1849	Pasteur becomes Professor of Chemistry at the University of Strasbourg. Marries Marie Laurent.
1850, 1851, 1853	Pasteur and his wife have a daughter, Jeanne; a son, Jean-Baptiste; and another daughter, Cécile.
1854	Pasteur becomes Professor of Chemistry and Dean of the Faculty of Sciences at Lille.
1855	Pasteur begins studies on fermentation.
1857	Pasteur becomes Administrator and Director of Scientific Studies at the Ecole Normale Supérieure.
1858, 1859, 1863	Daughter Marie Louise is born; daughter Jeanne dies; daughter Camille is born.
1859	Pasteur begins studies on Spontaneous Generation.
1861	Pasteur accidentally discovers anaerobic life.
1862	Pasteur is elected to the Academy of Sciences.
1863, 1864	Pasteur studies wine; he helps growers avoid having their wine spoil by using "pasteurization."
1865	Pasteur begins work on silkworm diseases; his father dies; daughter Camille dies. After reading Pasteur's writings, Dr. Joseph Lister pioneers antiseptic surgery in Scotland.
1866	Pasteur publishes a book on wine diseases and pasteurization. Daughter Cécile dies.
1868	Pasteur has a stroke, which results in a partial paralysis of his left side.
1870	Pasteur publishes a 2-volume book on silkworms.

1873	Pasteur is elected to the Academy of Medicine.
1877	Pasteur begins research on anthrax.
1878	Pasteur studies gangrene, septicemia, and childbirth fever.
1879	Pasteur and his assistants develop a chicken cholera vaccine. Daughter Marie Louise is married, as is son Jean-Baptiste.
1880	Pasteur begins work on rabies. His first grandchild, Camille Vallery-Radot, is born.
1881	Pasteur develops an anthrax vaccine and proves it works at a field trial in Pouilly le Fort.
1885	Nine-year-old Joseph Meister is successfully vaccinated with Pasteur's experimental rabies vaccine.
1886	Pasteur's grandson, Louis Pasteur Vallery-Radot, is born.
1886	The Pasteur Institute is inaugurated on November 14.
1892	France gives Pasteur a 70th birthday Jubilee celebration at the Sorbonne.
1895	Pasteur dies on September 28, at Chateau Villeneuve-l'Etang, near Paris.

RESOURCES

Bibliography

Louis Pasteur, by Richard Tames. New York: Franklin Watts, 1990.

Louis Pasteur: Founder of Microbiology, by Mary June Burton. New York: Franklin Watts, Inc., 1963.

Microbe Hunters, by Paul de Kruif. New Introduction by F. Gonzalez-Crussi. New York: Harcourt Brace (Harvest Paperback), 1996.

The Importance of Louis Pasteur, by Lisa Yount. San Diego: Lucent Books, 1994.

Websites

A major science website for young adults prepared by the American Library Association and which has more than 700 links is:
http://www.ala.org/parentspage./greatsites/science.html

The CDC (Center for Disease Control) offers a kid's Rabies Home Page that can be found at:
http://www.cdc.gov/ncidod/dvr/KIDSRABIES

The CDC also offers an environmental health website that can be viewed in either Engish or Spanish:
http://www.cdc.gov/Nceh/about/ncehKids/99kidsday/default.htm

The National Institutes of Health website links to a section containing medical and scientific information for young adults:
http://www.nih.gov

SciCentral provides a database of science sites, including sections for young adults:
http://www.scicentral.com

The American Museum of Natural History in New York offers two websites on epidemics and infectious diseases:
http://www.amnh.org/explore/infection/index.html
http://www.amnh.org/exhibitions/epidemic
The Discovery Channel offers "Epidemic—On the Trail of Killer Diseases" at:
http://www.discovery.com/exp/epidemic/epidemic.html

The United States Food and Drug Administration (FDA) offers a kids page on vaccines, disease prevention, etc., at:
http://www.fda.gov/oc/opacom/kids/default.htm

The United States Department of Agriculture offers Sci4Kids at:
http://www.ars.usda.gov/is/kids

A website called "Stalking the Mysterious Microbe" is available at:
http://www.microbe.org

Other Fun Websites

See the Microbe Zoo at:
http://www.commtechlab.msu.edu/sites/dlc-me/zoo
Live cells are at Cells Alive:
http://cellsalive.com
Check on bugs in the news at:
http://www.falcon.cc.ukan.edu/~jbrown/bugs.html
Dissect a virtual frog at:
http://www.curry.edschool.virginia.edu:80/~insttech/frog
or at:
http://www.george3.lbl.gov/vfrog

INDEX

Page numbers in italics refer to photographs or drawings.